Rattling Those Dry Bones

RATTLING
THOSE
DRY
BONES

WOMEN CHANGING THE CHURCH

EDITED BY JUNE STEFFENSEN HAGEN

3471

LuraMedia™

LuraMedia, Inc.
7060 Miramar Road, #104
San Diego, California 92121

Cover design by Dan Tollas, DeStijl Design, Doylestown, PA.
Printed on recycled paper.

Library of Congress Cataloging-in-Publication Data
Rattling those dry bones : women changing the Church / edited by June
    Steffensen Hagen.
        p.   cm.
    Includes bibliographical references.
    ISBN 0-931055-99-7
        1. Christian biography—United States. 2. Women in Christianity—
United States. I. Hagen, June Steffensen.
BR1713.R37   1995
277.3'0825'0922—dc20   94-40380
[B]   CIP

Grateful acknowledgment is made for permission to reprint the following copyrighted material:

Quotation from "On the Pulse of Morning" by Maya Angelou. Copyright © 1993 by Maya Angelou. Reprinted by permission of Random House, Inc.

Quotation from *Hopeful Imagination* by Walter Brueggemann. Copyright © 1986 by Fortress Press. Used by permission of Augsburg Fortress.

Quotation from *The Irrational Season* by Madeleine L'Engle. Copyright © 1977 by Crosswills Ltd. Reprinted by permission of HarperCollins Publishers, Inc.

Quotation from "The 23rd Psalm" by Bobby McFerrin. Copyright © 1990 Bobby McFerrin/Prob Noblem Music (BMI). All rights reserved. Reprinted by permission.

Quotations from *The Holographic Universe* by Michael Talbot. Copyright © 1990 by Michael Talbot. Reprinted by permission of HarperCollins Publishers, Inc.

Henry David Thoreau quotation from *Faith in a Seed*. Reprinted by permission of Island Press.

Quotation from *The Oath* by Elie Wiesel. Copyright © 1973 by Elie Wiesel. Reprinted by permission of Georges Borchardt, Inc. for the author.

Unless otherwise indicated, all biblical quotations are from the *New Revised Standard Version of the Bible*, © Copyright 1989, Division of Christian Education of the National Council of the Churches of Christ in the United States of America. Used by permission of the National Council of Churches of Christ in the United States of America.

New Jerusalem Bible (1985) quotations are used by permission of Doubleday, a Division of Bantam Doubleday Dell Publishing Group, Inc.

This book is dedicated to all
whose stories are yet untold.

CONTENTS

"The Lord gave the word;
great was the
company of women
who bore the tidings."

Psalm 68:11[1]

INTRODUCTION

June Steffensen Hagen, Editor

June Steffensen Hagen, Ph.D., is assistant professor of English, Bronx Community College of the City University of New York. She is the author of *Tennyson and His Publishers* (1979), editor of *Gender Matters: Women's Studies for the Christian Community* (1990), and writer of scholarly and personal essays. After more than twenty-five years as a literature professor in New York metropolitan area colleges and universities, she now functions as literary mid-wife via teaching writing and editing books. When June's not in a classroom or her study, she's usually in a rehearsal hall with the New York Choral Society or on the racquetball court or golf course. She cultivates her spiritual garden in the Episcopal church.

Y‍ou hold in your hand twenty-two personal essays by twenty-two remarkable women of faith. Each writes in response to the same set of questions; each approaches her subject from her own perspective; each tells her unique story. Yet all the essays have the possibility of sparking in you, at some point, the response, "Yes, I know what you mean — I've been there myself, but I never before read anyone who expressed what it was like," or "So *that's* what it was like for you! Your experience is very different from mine, but I loved hearing your story."

The book began out of my own curiosity. Because the past twenty years in the Christian church have been so tumultuous, especially with respect to women in leadership and all the related questions of "language, liturgy, and lethargy," as Sue Horner puts it in her essay (p. 73), I've wondered what's gone on in the inner spiritual lives of women at the front of the wedge. In fact, every time I read a book of feminist theology or hear a noted churchwoman speak at a conference, I want to ask certain questions, yet time seems too short, or perhaps I shy away from introducing the personal faith element into what is often a more esoteric or academic discussion. These questions probably have arisen in others as well; this book gives them voice.

Questions and Invitation

- *How did you get to where you are without losing heart?*
- *What holds you in the church?*
- *Who calls you to continue?*
- *What hope do you hold out for yourself and the church and other women in it?*
- *What words can you offer thoughtful Christian women who find the struggle continuing — and exhausting?*

With the encouragement of Lura Geiger, publisher, I drew up a list of more than seventy prominent women in Roman Catholic and Protestant churches, names drawn from my own reading and experience and from that of friends. I wrote to these women, asking the questions and inviting them to contribute their personal reflections. The invitation spelled out the intention of the volume:

> *We intend this collection to reach a wide audience of women, some active in the church, but some with one foot in the church's uncomfortable pew and the other stretching toward the door. Unfortunately, unless those in the latter group are readers of theology and biblical studies or fortunate enough to have run into your books and articles through friends, they may not understand that such discomfort is common and does not necessarily mean that one must take Mary Daly's route out that door. Autobiographical reflections on why you have stayed in the church, presented in an accessible volume, may help other women get their bearing in the church today.*

Exciting Results

The twenty-two essays chosen for the book turned out to do much more than I first expected. For example, when I used the manuscript in a study group in the small Catskill parish where my husband and I worship in the summer, I found that the men in the group found the essays as engaging as the women did. For example, John Edmonds wrote in his evaluation form,

> *Some of the authors raised issues which I resonated with, although I never thought of myself as much of a feminist; these related especially to marginality, oppression, and a vision of the church that is service- rather than power-oriented.*

Another participant, Mary Curtis, observed in an open letter to the authors that obvious points and central ideas are not always the most important part of a narrative:

> *Mostly, I think, it's the little insights into church and community life that kept me reading through — those little references and visions that tell me you've been the same places I've been, you've been frustrated and uplifted by the same people, the living saints of the church (warts and all) who work and laugh and*

argue and "get on with" worshiping communities. I'd like to be
able to take a week reading and studying each of your essays,
then sitting down with you and a few others to talk it through
to stretch our minds, to fuel us as we move back into the world.
Ah, what a luxury that would be!!

I felt that same excitement when I literally tore open the enve-
lopes as each essay came in the mail. I couldn't wait to see how those
questions were answered by people I had admired from afar but was
now getting the chance to read and work with firsthand. One of the
pleasures of doing all the editing chores, in fact, has been my
closeness to the text. Even when I move away from it, certain
moments or images or lines remain very vividly with me.

I see Madeleine L'Engle, Marie Fortune, Nancy Hardesty, and
Pamela Darling all sitting around a table, feasting, with Margaret
Guenther cajoling them in the words she heard in her own Eucharistic vision, "Have some more, darlings. There's plenty!" I see Shirley
Nelson dancing alone in her living room behind closed curtains. I
see Marjory Bankson as a high school girl practicing the pipe organ
in the mortuary and Laura Wright polishing the bear claw feet under
her mother's dining room table. I imagine Rosemary Haughton as a
young girl reading those two green cloth-covered books of saints'
lives. I celebrate Virginia Mollenkott's compelling dreams of Jesus.
Janet Ruffing's relief at finding the great mantle of mercy is palpable
to me.

But not all the vivid reminders are so pleasant. I also feel the
way the words to the usual he-man language hymns stuck in Joyce
Erickson's throat the day after she read Mary Daly's *Beyond God the
Father.* I weep with Ellen Kirby when her chance to weed the church
garden is denied her one early morning. Carmen Guerrero's graphic
retelling of a most horrible atrocity of the war in Bosnia is too
tormenting to ever forget.

The immediate situations of some writers also remain with me:
Anne Brown writing of radical trust and living with care as the rain
strikes the metal roof of her house in Vermont; Mary Hunt reflecting on the temptations of church position after preaching at the
Interfaith Healing Service for people with AIDS in Washington's

National Cathedral; Polly Wheat living in her polyglot New York City neighborhood and describing it as the external mirror of her many internal selves.

The vocational shifts and crisis situations of Elisabeth Moltmann-Wendel, Susan Cole, and Patricia Wilson-Kastner make this reader, at least, more aware than ever of what the latest pioneering generation of women in church leadership has endured.

And though I've never heard her preach, I hear Toinette Eugene's stirring words: "I say for women, for the weak, even for the wrong-headed, as well as for the discouraged and despairing in our midst — for all of us who truly want the Spirit to revive us again: 'God, you can make us live' " (p. 216).

That, expressed in many varied ways, is the tone underneath all these essays. The writers have been rattling the dry bones of the church because they ultimately trust in God's power to redeem and resurrect. But meanwhile they know that the stories we tell matter a great deal. "If enough women raise their voices in their own way and in their own place, changes will occur" (Horner, p. 73). The church needs to hear such voices — and the world, more importantly, *wants* to hear them. I hope, therefore, that all those reading this book will be encouraged to tell their own stories of faith.

June Steffensen Hagen

SECTION ONE

WRITERS

"The Almighty has given me
the gift of language,
and with it
will I offer praise to God."

Sirach 51:22[1]

Chapter 1
BONES

Madeleine L'Engle

Madeleine L'Engle is the noted author of *A Wrinkle in Time* (1962), *Arm of the Starfish* (1965), *Circle of Quiet* (1972), *Two-Part Invention* (1988), and many other widely read works of fiction and nonfiction for adults and children. *The Crosswicks Journals*, named after the country home in Connecticut where she and her late husband Hugh lived for so long, have allowed her readers an intimate sense of the person behind the publications. The recipient of nineteen honorary degrees, Madeleine has most recently written *Troubling a Star* (1994), *Certain Women*, and *A Rock That Is Higher* (both 1992). She conducts workshops and retreats all over the world and is a popular teacher of writing. Madeleine claims to be able to write *anywhere*!

The Lord said to Ezekiel,
"Prophesy to these bones, and say to them: O dry bones, hear the
word of the LORD. Thus says the Lord GOD to these bones: I
will cause breath to enter you, and you shall live. I will lay sinews
on you, and will cause flesh to come upon you, and cover you
with skin, and put breath in you, and you shall live; and you
shall know that I am the LORD." (Ezek. 37:4-6)

And so it happens. The bones are clothed with flesh; the Lord breathes life into them, and the dead bones live.

Ezekiel's book is indeed a wondrous one, but it falls into dust if I try to take it literally — not only the dry bones brought back to life but those marvelous twirling wheels covered with eyes. This book, like much of the Bible, demands that I understand it not only with my mind but also with my heart, with my imagination, with excitement.

And sometimes I think that excitement is the last thing that most people bring to the Bible and to church. How often do we go to church full of excitement, expectation, joy? How often are we willing to go to church to be changed?

Outside the Realm of Proof

This past winter during question-and-answer time at a large church where I had been giving several evening talks, I received two questions that have stuck with me. The first was: "Why are the sects growing in number, and why are the mainline churches losing members?" The answer seemed fairly simple. The mainline churches are not visible because they are not alight with faith and joy. People coming with questions, ultimate questions, are met with either evasions or finite answers. Even less helpful, the sects give finite answers to all the unanswerable questions. So many people, finding little joy in the church, turn to second best: what they perceive to be "absolute" answers. But absolute answers to the great unanswerable questions are basically deadly, and they may lead to such horrors as the mass suicides in Jonestown and Waco.

The second question was: "How can you, who are so open and full of excitement, still be part of an established church?" My answer was, "Some of us have to hang in there." And, "You can't change it from the outside."

Why? I sometimes ask myself. Why am I trying to hang in there, where I sometimes feel trapped between a wishy-washy liberalism where everything is permissible and a rigid fundamentalism where all questions are answered, all rules are absolute, and forgiveness is overruled by judgmentalism?

It was a woman who asked both questions, and I, who am a woman, found myself struggling with them long after the evening was over.

I had to look at my faith and understand that it is unreasonable and unprovable. We can neither prove nor disprove the existence of God. The Incarnation is so far outside the realm of proof that even looking for proof is laughable. One year my Christmas poem read:

This is the irrational season
When love blooms bright and wild.
Had Mary been full of reason
There'd have been no room for the child.[1]

The world around us wants reason, wants proof. Several people brought up in evangelical homes have told me of being given the image of the faith as a train, where the engine is the facts. What facts? There are no facts about God because facts are inadequate. We can look at the "facts" about the universe, which we believe to have been created by a beneficent God, but throughout the centuries these "facts" have changed as we have learned more. We have moved from the understanding of Abraham, where the world was indeed the center of the universe, with the sun, the moon, and the stars put in the sky for our benefit, to our present understanding of a universe so enormous that even the highest mathematical minds cannot comprehend its size. A galaxy has now been discovered that is something like several trillion billion light years away. And at the same time, we are struggling to understand the infinitely small world of subatomic particles, as much smaller than we are as galaxies are larger than we are.

Probably our present understanding of the universe is as far from the "facts" of creation as Abraham's was. I am fascinated by the present theories because they seem to imply a God of magnificent power and glory, but I do not trust them as absolute facts. The theories lead me to marvel at the God of such awesomeness being willing to come live with us "in human vesture," in the ordinary, finite human body of Jesus of Nazareth.

The only "facts" we have about this Jesus come from a history written about two thousand years ago by one Josephus, who mentioned that there was a man called Jesus who was crucified — and even this mention is not considered totally authentic. If we have to depend on "facts" in order to put life on the dry bones of the churches, we are doomed to failure.

Love Beyond Reason

Children are better believers than adults, and women are better believers than men because women have been allowed throughout the centuries to remain in touch with the nurturing, the tender, the artistic, and the unreasonableness of love. We love our children because we love them, because we have birthed them, because they are. We love our friends and lovers not necessarily because they are handsome or brilliant or wealthy but because something indefinable in them reaches out to us and causes our hearts to open to them. On the other hand, we have been trained by society for centuries to look for finite answers, no matter how infinite the question. We have been taught that all of life, including faith, should be reasonable.

But life is not reasonable. Nor is faith. Perhaps even creation is not reasonable. Why should there be something instead of nothing? Even the great physicist Stephen Hawking admits he cannot answer this question. God is love, and it is the nature of love to create. That's not a particularly rational reason, but as far as I'm concerned, it's as good as any.

As a woman, despite my classical liberal arts education, I have managed to understand that the unreasonable and unprovable are as real as the reasonable and provable. So, rather than being envious of men, and brittle about them, I believe that women need to be tender and sensitive and willing to try to help men into the wider, more wonderful, and exciting world that we have not had to abandon.

But this is scary! This wide world includes unanswerable questions. This thrilling world includes a Maker who gave up dominion and power for love of us stiff-necked people.

In my mind's ear, I hear God saying to God: "Can I do it? Can I give up my galaxies, my solar systems, my hydrogen clouds and comets? Can I leave it all and become a zygote, a powerless, thoughtless, insignificant seed in the womb of a young woman? Can I be born as a human baby, into human mortality, and die as any human creature dies? Can I do it? Do I love them that much?"

It is my faith, not my reason, that tells me that the answer is Yes! How do we understand this kind of love? Does it make a demand of us that we are not ready to meet? Are we, too, called to love this much?

The God I worship is a God of love, not punishment. I am amazed at the number of people — and this includes women as well as men — who visualize God as Moses, and Moses in a very bad temper, at that. This God is *Out To Get Us*! if we do not continually placate the old gent by winning more and more merit badges.

This masculine, anthropomorphic God has been around in too many churches for too long and has led to such unhappy theories as Anselm's substitutionary atonement, which, when pushed to where it logically leads, says that Jesus Christ came to save us from an angry father who can't forgive us unless his only son gets crucified. Or more bluntly put, Jesus had to come to save us from God the Father. This, I understand, is taught in some churches, but I find it incompatible with a God of love, and it is a God of love I believe in.

"Atonement," by the way, means exactly what the word says: At-one-ment — at least, that is what two etymological dictionaries tell me. There is nothing in the word of sacrifice. It may well be that it is through Jesus that we, too, are made "at one" with God, but we are at one with a God of love, not a God who is ready to damn us to hell if we deviate from the straight and narrow path. Oh, yes, you can find proof of this punitive God in the Bible, just as you can find proof of the loving God in the Bible, just as you can find proof of almost anything you want to prove in the Bible. But I am far more interested in love than proof.

Where else does all this proving lead? To a God who loves only Christians, and only certain kinds of Christians? For how many centuries have many Protestants believed that Catholics are not Christians, and vice versa? How many churches still hold "closed Communion," allowing only certain Christians to come to God's table. It is *God's* table. What gives us the right to check the guest list?

And where else does it lead? It leads to a literal and unimaginative reading of Scripture that has allowed "us" to take over the land of others because God wants us to have the heathens' land because we are his people and they are not. "His." This God is a tribal, male god indeed.

It leads to a Christianity of exclusivity, which is contrary to what I read in the Gospels, where Jesus is constantly throwing out exclusivity in favor of inclusivity. Who are his protagonists? Others. Not "us." Women. Samaritan women, yet. Samaritan lepers. Samaritans who are more compassionate than the good Jews. Syro-Phoenician women. Tax collectors. We hear the stories so often that they lose their sharp edges and become so blunted that we forget what they are really about.

A Thin, Humorless Church

There are times when it seems that awe at the Incarnation and the love of God is not enough to make one a Christian. One has to believe — or not believe — in all kinds of ridiculous little laws. For example, in the Articles of Religion in the Historical Documents section of the Episcopal *Book of Common Prayer*, we are told that we are not permitted to believe in purgatory — because this is a Roman Catholic belief. Obviously, this was written before O'Hare Airport was built! I find purgatory a useful image and comfort myself every time I have to change planes at O'Hare that at least a few days will be lopped off my time in purgatory.

Sometimes we are not even allowed to laugh. Alas.

When I am asked if I am "religious," I have to ask, does that mean "narrow-minded, exclusive, full of answers"? When I am asked if I am a Christian, I have to ask, does that mean that God loves only Christians? And, within Christendom, only certain denominations?

What is the fear I find in so many churches, including my own? Fear of others, fear of differences of opinion, differences in our expressions of faith, fear of God? Where there is fear, there is not love, and where there is not love, there is not God.

If I have to believe in a Christianity of facts, I cannot be a Christian. There are a few people, of course, who are convinced from my books that I am not a Christian. By far the majority of people who graciously write to me are affirming and loving and positive, but there are a few, fortunately proportionately a very few, who want my books, particularly the fantasies, removed from the library shelves. A few would like to convert me to a Christianity of facts. A few would prefer to damn me to hell. But who, except God, knows our hearts? Knows whether or not we are truly "Christian"? Who knows what "Christian" means?

There are days when I am confronted by a thin, humorless church, and I wonder how long I can hang in there.

Can These Dry Bones Live Again?

So, can anything be done? Can these dry bones live again? Yes, but it's going to take courage, sacrifice, accusations of heresy, and enduring all the narrow-mindedness that makes us want to withdraw. But if I withdraw, if I turn away from those who demand factual answers, then I am turning away from the broken body of which I am a part and excluding myself from the ultimate party, where all God's children will gather together to make merry.

All I can do, all I am trying to do, is to go on writing what I feel called to write. I can try to go on hanging in there, with all my faults and flaws, and with all my womanhood. For God's sake (truly!), let us be women.

What I want ordained women to do is to be women, to bring the female part of the human being back into the church. The masculine part is already there, and I do not want to dispose of it. We need both, and we need them to love each other, to "know" each other, to marry. We need to offer love instead of coercion. The secular world, not without cause, has been frightened of the Judeo-Christian tradition largely because literalists have denied the imagination and clouded their vision of the Maker.

Tradition and Struggle

Tradition is important to me. But in my own life, traditions have had to change, to be renewed, rediscovered. New traditions have had to replace old ones. When our children left the nest, the tradition of the family around the table, together, for dinner, had to change. The dinner table is important, and the tradition of lighted candles, a well-set table, food prepared with love has remained, but the people around the table vary with what is going on in my life.

And I look back in history to another tradition of my Southern family: All children born on this land, white or black, slave or free, deserved to be taught to read and write. That was a good tradition. To educate slaves was extraordinarily liberal at that time in history. But they had not yet made the next step in their thinking: Slavery is intolerable.

As they learned to question their culture, we in our time are learning to question the tradition of a male-dominated church. It is about time, and the questions need to continue. But asking questions doesn't mean that all traditions need to be discarded. In my apartment building in New York, in December we have beautiful lighted Christmas trees in our lobby; we also have a Menorah in the great entrance windows for Hanukkah candles. At this time we would be allowed to display neither in a public place. I live in a tenant-owned-and-managed building, which gives us a freedom tenants in landlord-owned buildings do not have. It has been pointed out that teachers may talk about safe sex and make condoms available in public schools, but they may not pray aloud themselves or allow their students to pray aloud. Something is skewed. Something is broken. Those bones won't have life breathed into them again until the radical love God has given us, all of us, is accepted once more.

I am a struggling Christian, and I am far more comfortable with strugglers from other traditions than I am with Christian literalists.

I have friends who are observant Jews, Mormons, Baptists, Buddhists, friends of many nationalities, races, and religions. What we have in common with each other (rather than our religious affiliations) is that we are still willing to ask questions, to learn from each other, to hope for deeper understanding, and to love. I want to learn as much as I can from all sources — scientific, religious, and even secular — what *have* we Christians done to produce so much secularism? I want to learn from the so-called "primitive" religions of Native Americans, Aborigines, Maoris. What I learned fifty years ago from some farmers' wives with their ancient lore has been invaluable to me all my life.

We live on what has indeed become a very small planet. If we don't learn from each other, if we don't learn how to live together, if we don't learn to accept what is best in each other, we are lost.

One of my favorite "saints" is George MacDonald. He was excommunicated from his denomination because he could not believe that a God of love would ignore or condemn two-thirds of the people on the planet — who, after all, were made by God. George MacDonald, in photographs, has a big, bushy beard, but to me he is a "female" icon, for his love was nurturing, tender, maternal. I don't want a god who loves only a few people, either.

We have moved in our thinking a long way from some of the ways of looking at God in the early chapters of Scripture because our knowledge of God's universe has been vastly enlarged. We make a terrible mistake in trying to look at such nomadic protagonists as Abraham and Sarah as though they lived at the end of the nineteenth century. We can't rewrite the Bible (though there have been some foolish attempts to contort it into justifications of our own unloving actions), but we can look at it in its own historical context and not view Abraham as though he ought to understand contemporary astrophysics, an overpopulated planet, and all that has happened in the past three thousand or more years since God promised him that he would be the father of nations. Abraham did not know that the stars are suns, giant atomic furnaces, that there are more galaxies than any scientist can count, that the world of the microcosm, the world of subatomic particles, is as vast as the macrocosm. He did not know about DNA or antibiotics or open-heart surgery. He did understand famine, and that people were born, lived their lives, and then died. He did know that he was personally connected to and committed to the God who made him, and who loved him, no matter how many mistakes he made. He even chided God, "Shall not the Judge of all the earth do right?" (Gen. 18:25).

Ezekiel (how, how do we understand this great prophet in a literal way?) did not put flesh and bones and blood back on those dry bones, nor could he breathe life into them. God did. God who is creator, lover, joy-giver. God who calls on us to be co-creators, to be lovers, to give joy. Throughout history most of the people God has called on to do the work of love have been misunderstood, ostracized, punished, crucified. That is usually the price. But it is worth it.

Madeleine L'Engle

Chapter 2
PROSPECTING

Shirley Nelson

Shirley Nelson, now living in Albany, New York, holds a master's degree in writing from the State University of New York. She is the author of two award-winning books. Her novel, *The Last Year of the War* (1978; 1989), captures a little-examined American religious experience: the evangelical Christian college subculture and its effect on the life of the mind and the life of faith. Her second book, *Fair, Clear and Terrible: The Story of Shiloh, Maine* (1989), is a documented account of a turn-of-the-century religious extremist movement in which Shirley's parents grew up and her uncle lost his life. She has also published articles, reviews, and fiction in a wide variety of periodicals and anthologies (*Christian Century, Family Circle, Image*). She speaks at schools, workshops, and churches, and is presently at work on another novel.

*I*n the summer of 1849, my great-grandfather, Hiram White, a red-bearded blacksmith from Maine, invested all his savings to sail around Cape Horn to California. There he staked a gold-mining claim far up the Feather River above the town of Sacramento. He was twenty-seven, single, and full of brawn. For many months he worked the claim, battling grizzly bears, robbers, and lice, finding hardly enough gold to justify his labors. Finally, wasted by dysentery, he sold the claim for a fraction of its cost and took to the sea for a cure, working aboard ship for $10 a day. Back home at last with $1,000 in his pocket, he learned that the two men to whom he had sold the claim had already netted more than half a million dollars and were still going strong. Hiram returned to blacksmithing, got married, and fathered a houseful of children.

All in the Family

That story flies into my mind as I contemplate my history in the church, though I'm not sure why. I could be tempted, I suppose, to use it as a metaphor. It could be said that I have invested my "life savings" in the church since I first joined it as a teenager fifty years ago, or that I've faced obstacles and pestilence in order to mine my claim, not always sure that the ore I extract is truly gold. A self-dramatizing analogy, to say the least, and like most analogies accurate only in part — even less so if I press the application. For have I abandoned my claim? Sold out too quickly? Suffered great loss? Or hung on through thick and thin to strike at last the gleaming lode that has filled my life with riches? It will never do.

My inclination anyway these days is to reach for simple, straightforward answers. Why am I still in the church? "Because I want to be, that's all," I can hear myself saying — not to be flippant, but to disarm the need for any elaboration or defense. I present no convincing rationale, that answer says, no vindication, no gloss, no twelve steps to glory. The Apostle Peter may have been "ready always" to give his answer (1 Peter 3:15, KJV), but I bet there were times when even he chose silence and simply drew a fish in the sand. In fact, as time goes by, my preference to remain in the church has become so mixed with the layers of my life that it may be impossible to explain. It seems better to say that I just can't help it. Perhaps it's something in my genes.

That, at least, is a place to begin. As biological science it may not hold up, but it's certainly true that my connections to the church began long before I was born. And that, of course, brings us in a short full circle directly back to my ancestors. Not that any of them made a mark. We're not talking about George Whitefield here, or Jonathan Edwards, or any of the strong, radical women who hassled the mainstream church: Anne Hutchinson, Mother Ann Lee, Susan B. Anthony. The most notorious of my forebears was Ephraim Stinchfield, a somewhat uncouth man, I gather, with a name I happily did not inherit. Ephraim was famous only within a two-hundred-mile radius in the hills of southern Maine early in the nineteenth century. He was a self-appointed evangelist in a tiny sect called the Freewill Baptists, one of many groups that separated from Puritan bureaucracy. Ephraim was a farmer, an ordinary citizen without ambition. A calling to preach was hardly expected. One day as he rode horseback alone through the wilderness, the lost souls of the towns around him appeared like Ezekiel's vision of the valley of dry bones. "With my hands upon my loins," his memoir reads, "I cried as I rode . . . as loud as the strength of my lungs would permit, can these dry bones live?" He repeated the question, shouting into the woods, until at length an answer flashed into his mind with a power he was unable to resist: "Prophesy, son of man!"

Without education or training, he blundered his way through sermon after sermon, and though people actually begged him to desist, he preached four thousand times in a decade and added one thousand baptized souls to the Freewill rolls, including a 95-year-old woman who was immersed in a river in November and survived to do her own shouting.

I will say this about Ephraim, however much I want to distance myself from his embarrassing zeal: He knew what it meant to be suddenly, irreversibly transformed, and to the best of what lay within him gave his life to his Transformer. For this reason, he'd have been saddened if he had lived long enough to witness the cynicism of his grandson, Hiram White, the prospector for gold. Hiram was self-declared too — an atheist, or at least that was his public stance. He refused to belong to the church. Invited one day by a Freewill elder to get down on his knees and "settle this thing right now," Hiram replied that he would rather burn in hell than follow such a lead.

A Mix of Many Parts

But take another look. All along, Hiram had been attending that same little church every single Sunday morning for two long hours, occupying a "singer's seat" (he had a fine tenor voice), with one of the smaller of his eight children on his knee. He belonged after all, while he fiercely protected his right to heed the counsel of his own inclinations.

And then there was Hiram's son, Wendell, my father's father, a Maine dairy farmer and erstwhile teacher, discontented with the church as he knew it, discontented with American politics, discontented with himself. Wendell brought his wife and four half-grown children to Shiloh Hilltop, a nearby community in possession of the Whole Truth, the real and only Apostolic Church in the world, the pure Remnant, the Bride of Christ preparing for the return of the Bridegroom. For this movement he gave up everything and risked the lives and health of his children.[1]

But however misguided Wendell may have been, when at the end of sixteen years at Shiloh the great plan crumbled in disgrace and he was forced to begin life all over again, he did it without bitterness, blaming no one but himself.

Unfortunately, I can't speak of the women in this genealogy. Hiram's wife Susan is an exception. She made a name for herself with her tongue. A weighty abolitionist who saw as her Christian and womanly duty participation in all political discussions within earshot, Susan could argue down any man in town who dared to debate her convictions, and she did so without reticence or apology.

This is my father's family tree. My intention is not to show favor toward the patriarchal side. It's simply that the record there is more available, which may mean only that they talked a lot. As for my father, the last of the males bearing the family name, he brought up the end of the line in a lifelong flight from the "unperturbèd pace" of the Hound of Heaven.

I embody all the parts of this mixture: Ephraim's incongruous call, Hiram's fortress of doubt, Susan's clamorous demand for equity, Wendell's cry for utopian fulfillment, and my father's belabored agnosticism. All of them had one thing in common — personal responsibility for their own beliefs. None of them wavered before the illusion of choice, and while some at least nodded to overarching grace, they would surely scoff at my genes theory or the evasion of duty in "I can't help it." Don't count on *me* for those genes, they would say. You can help it, all right. And you had better help it, for you and you alone are accountable for the disposition of your own heart and mind.

That was the Freewiller position, too. No mother or daddy church to carry you through when you mess things up. It's you and God first and foremost, with nobody in the wings to whisper the cues. Though I give a big nod to the illusion of choice and fall on my face in need of that overarching grace, the sense of responsibility is deep in my bones, and personal one-on-one with God operates as a core of reality for me.

No Retreating

Consequently, what I mean by "church" most naturally is not a local church or denomination but the rangy, uncorporate, invisible body of Christ, to which one may belong without joining the visible institution. It took me a long time to recognize the necessity for the corporate body, a concrete home for the awesome mystery of God at work in the world. I've learned to respect the potential of checks and balances offered by the authority of that palpable presence — that is, when the authority "is critically open to the possibility of its own transformation," as Elisabeth Schüssler Fiorenza has said.[2] Though the hazards lurking in the exercise of any authority have been exhibited painfully throughout history, I believe that the invisible church, swimming about in its essential freedom, needs a point of focus more than ever. This is especially so because of the sort of hard-headed individualism demonstrated by my own heritage, where the monsters of ideology wait to be spawned.

What's more, I've learned that if I belong to the visible church, then I am also visible, whether or not I'm in the mood. No retreating into a private, none-of-the-world's-business kind of faith. If I call myself a Christian, then I must be one openly, even during the periods of dryness, when there seems no rational or existential justification for such a perspective in the world. Or when I feel only shame and despair at the church's failures, or my own. Even then I can't retreat from confrontation. If I belong to this vast family, I belong, and there is no escape from engagement. All the goofy cousins are mine, the uncles who drink too much and feel you up, the grandpas who rule with their canes, the great-aunts who stuff you with sweets, the sister who bosses you around, and the parents who give and take excessively. I may disagree with them from the bottom of my soul, weep at their tragic decisions, fight them in private and public, and even call the cops, but I can never kid myself into thinking that I'm not connected. They are still my family. "The eye cannot say to the hand, 'I have no need of you' " (1 Cor. 12:21).

And no doubt I'm a nerdy cousin, too, and who else other than my family will tell me so? Who else really worries about me, allows me to sulk and shut myself in my room, kick the door and yell, and still come out for dinner? That may not be everyone's experience in the church, but it's been mine, that I still belong no matter how much at odds I may be with the rest of the family.

A Preposterous Hope

"A mature Christianity . . . is one in which our understanding of our interrelatedness has come to full development," says Elizabeth O'Connor, referring to Ephesians 4:16.[3] That kind of adult completeness eludes us. It comes and goes in fragments. I've seen it in dozens of congregations I've never joined but to which in my universal membership I still belong, those who have been clear-eyed and courageous in crucial circumstances. I think, for example, of the Dexter Avenue Baptist Church in Montgomery, Alabama, headquarters for the Montgomery bus boycott in 1955. I think of South-side Presbyterian Church in Tucson, Arizona, which in similar acts of civil disobedience gave sanctuary to illegal immigrants. I think of Our Lady of Solentiname, the Christian base community in Nicaragua where the gospel meant Good News for the poor in the face of military oppression.

These are not perfect churches, but they represent the *possibilities*, and that is what we share. The odds are not what matter. We try and fail and try again, slowly learning what it means to believe and live the gospel. Where else but in the church of Christ can we practice what the world can't comprehend — the "non-sense" of the Prodigal Son, the Widow's Mite, the Good Samaritan, and the notion of losing our lives to find them. Where else can we explore the intricacies of applying that law of love, without silliness and naïveté, until, to paraphrase Reinhold Niebuhr, the law of love becomes the ultimate measure of justice throughout the world.[4]

It's a preposterous hope. But hope, like responsibility, is what we can't relinquish. We could call it "prospecting." Maybe that word is all I can wrest from my great-grandfather's California adventure, but it seems like enough. It means acting in faith. I like that better than knowing beyond all doubt that the gold is there and easily extracted. This above all is what the world has trouble understanding, that we would be willing to bet our lives on the outrageous treasure of the gospel.

I suppose the Apostle Peter, the talker, might see this as a fairly full answer, after all. That doesn't make me worry less about our reliance on words to recognize our motives. Even "because I want to" seems wordy to me at times.

I remember a night some thirty years ago. The children, all small, were asleep, and my husband was not at home. For months I had been feeling an emptiness, the natural result (I knew) of a long, slow separation from the comfortable context and language of what it had meant for me to be a Christian. The separation was deliberate and necessary for growth, but I'd come to the point where the void needed filling. Someone had given us a recording of a folk mass, a new thing at the time. I played it three times that night while I danced alone in the living room with the curtains drawn shut. I didn't tell myself that this was the most primitive form of worship known to humanity. I didn't say a thing. I just danced.

When I was done, I knew I had reached one of those way-stations that are so wonderfully provided when we need them most on this crazy journey — a place to begin again, this time on my feet, with no analysis or explanation required.

And, as a matter of fact, that seems the perfect way to end this discourse, with a "wordless" statement, you could say, or better yet a fish, just two intersecting lines in the sand.

Shirley Nelson

Chapter 3

THE COMMUNION OF SAINTS AND SINNERS

Nancy A. Hardesty

Nancy A. Hardesty, Ph.D., is currently visiting associate professor of religion at Clemson University. She lives in Greenville, South Carolina. Nancy is one of the founders of the Evangelical and Ecumenical Women's Caucus and of *Daughters of Sarah*, a Christian feminist magazine. With Letha Dawson Scanzoni, she wrote the early feminist classic *All We're Meant to Be: Biblical Feminism for Today* (1974; third edition, 1992). Nancy has also written *Inclusive Language in the Church* (1986) and *Women Called to Witness: Evangelical Feminism in the Nineteenth Century* (1984). She says she collects marbles against the day when she begins to lose hers.

Why, after fifty years, am I still in the church? Certainly the church — or perhaps I should say various churches — have tried to run me off. I was born into a church-going family, and I was only weeks old when my mother bundled me up and took me to our little country Methodist church. I grew up in that church. My fondest memories are of my parents' Sunday school class suppers in the basement. Such feasts!

Easter Day 1949 I was baptized there, the drops of water running down through the straw and flowers of my tiny hat. The minister had come to our house and explained the significance of the sacrament and the responsibilities of joining the church. Our family joined together. I knew what I was doing.

But when I was ten, we moved to the city. There I knew that my maternal grandparents had left the "apostate" Methodist church down the street where my paternal grandparents and my father had attended when he was a boy. A brave band of believers had left Methodism to found a Christian and Missionary Alliance Church (C&MA). Their first pastor was Miss Marvin.

One night, October 22, 1951, my grandmother asked me if I wanted to pray with her and be saved. I said I did. I publicly professed my faith later that winter during citywide revival meetings at the Memorial Auditorium. The C&MA said my Methodist sprinkling was not good enough; I must be immersed. And so I was. I joined the church and became a fundamentalist.

When I went off to Wheaton College in Illinois, there was no C&MA church in town. My freshman year I dutifully attended Wheaton Bible Church. The college Sunday school class was taught by a Greek professor from Moody Bible Institute, and I took copious notes. My sophomore year I visited every church in town on Sunday mornings, but Sunday evenings I soon settled into a pattern of evensong at the local Episcopal church. The service was ethereal and afterward over coffee and cookies one or another of the professors from Seabury-Western Theological Seminary discussed the faith. From my junior year on, I also went there every Sunday morning. I said I had been aesthetically deprived as a child. I yearned to be part of a truly historic faith, and I wanted a church that was at least trying to grapple with the intensifying social problems of the 1960s.

My parents were alarmed. I went to journalism school at Northwestern University and hung out at the local Canterbury House. When I wrote home that I was going to be confirmed as an Episcopalian at the end of May, my father wrote me for the first time ever to say he was very hurt and very angry and intended to disown me. But he didn't, and for more than twenty-five years I was an Episcopalian — in Chicago, Philadelphia, Atlanta.

Growing up in the C&MA, I had heard the call of God to serve, and I responded. Although there were no more Miss Marvins pastoring local churches in the U.S., there were lots of women missionaries. And our pastors informed us that unless God told us specifically otherwise, God was calling us to be missionaries. I was to be a missionary teacher. My pleased pastor introduced me to visiting missionaries, who smiled approvingly. Until my senior year in high school. Then they started saying, "We'll be happy to see you on the field once you're married."

I was crushed. I was only seventeen, and I was already in despair because there was no one to date. After all we were the only "true Christians," and we were not to be "unequally yoked together with unbelievers" (2 Cor. 6:14, KJV). But in our small congregation there were only two boys my age, one of whom was already in reform school.

In college I lost interest in becoming a teacher and decided instead to become a Christian journalist. On my first job I realized that the woman who was my boss had been passed over several times for the position of managing editor. My second editor put it succinctly: "How many women editors do you know?" The publisher told me that it was "good stewardship of God's money" to pay me less than a man with fewer qualifications. I became a feminist.

When the Episcopal church voted in 1976 to ordain women as priests, I knew I was called to seek ordination. The diocese had a year-long program called "Experiment in Ministry." We first met at a weekend retreat in February with the bishop and other leaders of the church. The bishop welcomed us and spoke of spirituality and God's calling. We were the largest group of candidates to date, twenty-four men and women eager to test our vocation to priesthood.

We were divided into two groups, twelve each. In June we started ministering in the alcohol rehabilitation unit of a mental hospital. The first afternoon the bishop came and spoke: "As I said in February, only three people will be chosen as candidates, but I hope this won't become competitive." Perhaps I should not have pointed out that he had said nothing in February about choosing only three.

Our group was led by two men totally devoid of skill in group dynamics (the bishop later testified under oath that he had been misled about their qualifications). Taking their lead from Freud, they simply sat back and observed as the group disintegrated. One woman had a complete emotional breakdown and was hospitalized. One man toyed with suicide, another took to heavy drinking. We never discussed spirituality or our sense of God's call. After nine months, no one in our group was recommended for priesthood. The only person from our group who did become a priest several years later was the youngest and most immature member, a man who had told us he preferred rocks to people. When the group had tried to confront him with his anger, he had stormed out of the room and never completed the "required" program. But then his parents were members of a large church, and his father, a physician, was a substantial donor.

They told me that they didn't think I was suitable for the priesthood because I was overweight and had unresolved sexual issues. Of course, we had never discussed my weight or my sexual issues. I was thirty-seven, and I had resolved my sexual issues, but they did not want to hear about it.

I felt as though I had followed God's leading right into a cul-de-sac. The call to ordination was definitely gone, but I tried to stay within the church. And I did, for a while.

I have always been aware that the church includes sinners as well as saints. As a child I understood that my Sunday school teacher had been caught by her husband in the hayloft of her barn with the father of the little boy I liked. I did not know what they were doing up there, but I understood it was wrong. I also knew that the most conservative, evangelical, fundamentalist of all our Methodist pastors had run away with the piano player at his next church, leaving a wife and four children to cope on their own.

At one of the Christian magazines I worked for, the treasurer demanded hugs and kisses before he would hand over our paychecks. We did not call it sexual harassment back then; I just felt queasy.

But after I was rejected for priesthood, I sometimes attended a church in a growing part of town with a friend who served there as a seminarian. The priest was young and dynamic. But then strange things started to happen. He convinced the vestry to renovate the sanctuary, turning the cruciform church around so that the altar faced west. He omitted the Lord's Prayer from the service and stumbled over the words of the Nicene Creed. One night at dinner in a fine restaurant with a small group of parishioners, he began teasing one of the women in a way that had screaming sexual overtones. Suddenly he turned to me and, in a crackling voice, asked, "What do you want more than anything else in the world? I can give it to you."

I knew I wanted to be ordained, but I also knew I had just heard the voice of Satan, alive and in person. I replied as I knew I must, "You do not have that power!" But I sensed that indeed in that diocese he just might.

The next day the woman confessed to the seminarian that the priest had been trying to initiate an affair with her, that he had been terrorizing her and her family, and that she was sure he had killed her dog. The seminarian reported immediately to the bishop. The suffragan bishop was sent to investigate, and he found Communion hosts desecrated, processional crosses upended, and the ashes of a parishioner buried beneath the new altar. The priest threatened to kill the bishop and was admitted to a psychiatric hospital, but within two weeks he had talked his way out. The bishop reinstated him in the parish and eventually found him a fine job in another diocese. The bishop said he did not believe in evil and certainly not in demon possession.

The bishop then dismissed the seminarian who had brought the matter to his attention. She sued. It was an eerie feeling for me to know that I was being followed at night by a detective hired by my own bishop.

Still, I tried to stay within the church. At this time I was active in another parish as well, reading Scripture, giving Communion, serving on the vestry. The pastor and I had talked many times about my grief and confusion over not being recommended for ordination, about my spiritual struggles, and about my despair over the lack of fulfillment in my personal and sexual relationships. I had been in his home, with his wife and family on numerous social occasions.

One day he called and asked if we could have lunch together. Over a table at Denny's, he said, "I have a big favor to ask. Could I use your house on Thursday afternoons?"

"For what?" I asked naively.

At first I didn't get it. I finally realized that he was already having an affair and wanted to conduct it in my bed on Thursday afternoons.

It was two years before I set foot in a church again.

Eventually I became hungry for the Eucharist. I knew I could find it anonymously at the five o'clock service at the Roman Catholic cathedral. It was an informal folk mass, and nobody asked questions. It met my needs, but soon I realized that, while I enjoyed the service, these were not "my people." Their words were not *The Book of Common Prayer* I had memorized. I could never accept their theology, their hierarchy.

I returned to an Episcopal church I had attended when I first came to the city. I went as I needed to — at 8 a.m. or 6 p.m. on Sunday, or the 7 a.m. healing service on Wednesdays. I kept a fairly low profile. But at least I felt welcome. The language was becoming more inclusive, and a surplus of nonstipendiary priests at that time meant that there was often a woman somewhere within the chancel.

One evening the associate priest, whom I had known for about ten years by now, said, "You've been looking rather happy for the past few weeks. You must be in love!"

"Yes," I admitted.

"With a man or a woman?" he asked.

I laughed and answered, "With a woman." He made coming out so easy. My partner and I always felt welcome there. When my home was destroyed by fire, the rector came to bless the rebuilt house, to celebrate a mass with a circle of our friends, and to bless the rings symbolizing our relationship.

The rector had never married; he lived with his mother and collected antiques. I liked him, despite his obstinate streak. I became a licensed layreader again, reading the lessons, serving Communion, assisting at the altar. As before, I usually volunteered for the more marginal services, but I was content. Then one day all layreaders were summoned to a meeting after the 11 a.m. service. Half of us came. The rector exploded in anger, lashing out for half an hour at "irresponsible" people who did not fulfill their duties, declaring that the bishop had invested him with authority over us, and he was going to enforce that authority, and if we didn't do what we were told and come when we were assigned, he would tear up our licenses. I was there. I had never missed an assigned service unless I had arranged for a substitute. And I was a *volunteer*; this was not my paid employment. I was stunned. I was in shock. I cried for three days. I knew I was overreacting, but I had been reinjured in some deep place where I had been abused before. I never trusted him or respected him in the same way again.

When I moved to South Carolina in 1988, I did not seek out an Episcopal church. South Carolina was, and is, a very conservative diocese; no women were then ordained, and few have been since. And in the South, the Episcopal church is definitely the church of the elite: Pentecostals and independent Baptists are working class; Methodists, Presbyterians, and Southern Baptists are middle class; the Episcopalians once owned the mills the others worked in. I am old enough now to know that my aspirations to middle-class status are sustained only by my education, not my income.

Rather, I became a member of the Metropolitan Community Church of Greenville. MCC is a national denomination founded in 1968 with an intentional ministry welcoming gay and lesbian people. They welcomed me and needed me. It was a five-year-old congregation with an average attendance of less than twenty. They asked me to preach, and they invited me to celebrate the Eucharist. All of my gifts, as well as my tithes, were welcomed and accepted. Since then, we have grown to a congregation averaging fifty. We support a full-time pastor. God has not renewed my call to ordained ministry, but I have claimed my own authority to preach, teach, consecrate, bless, and anoint. I also serve on the board of directors. My congregation, my community affirms my ministry.

Of course, there have been bumps along the way. We called one pastor who seemed ideal until I found out that he was deliberately dividing the congregation, telling newcomers that I and another male leader were witches and that inclusive language was an evil plot.

Why am I still in the church and why do I stay? Communion. One word says it all. First of all, Holy Communion, the Lord's Supper, Eucharist. The sacrament nurtures me, nourishes me, heals me, and sustains my intimacy with God. I need it. I also need the communion involved in being in a local church with a group of other Christians. At times we wear on each other's last nerve. They don't always do what I think they should, and they agree I get on my high horse too often. We love each other and try to support each other when life gets rough. None of us is perfect, and most of us have been around each other long enough to know it and learn to ignore it.

All of this, of course, is to say nothing of the depths of racism, sexism, and heterosexism embodied in the church's sources, history, theology, and institutional structures. My academic work in Bible and church history has made me painfully aware of the pervasive problems.

Given my personal history, I often feel that I am clinging to faith by the very tips of my fingernails. And then I am socked in the stomach by one more pronouncement that women can't be ministers because all of Jesus' disciples were men, or that homosexual people will not inherit the kingdom of God because Paul said so, or that God created women subordinate to men, or that America is God's country so we can bomb any nation we dislike.

I feel myself begin to swing, and I ask myself why I bother to cling. And I remind myself that I cling not to a book and not to a bunch of bigots' interpretations. I cling to a Person and to a people.

Charles Williams, in *Descent of the Dove: A Short History of the Holy Spirit* and in the novel *Descent into Hell*, speaks of co-inherence, his view of the communion of the saints.[1] He reminds me that I am in communion with Christ and with the saints of history and the present. In Christ we are a living organism, one body. And I know that in God I live and move and have my being.

Nancy A. Hardesty

Chapter 4

THE FIRE OF HOLINESS

Rosemary Haughton

Rosemary Haughton lives and works at Wellspring House in Gloucester, Massachusetts. Founded in 1981, this community has gained respect for its pioneer work with the homeless, for low-income housing, and in education on an empowerment model in economic development. In 1974 she, her husband, and others founded a community in southwest Scotland, called Lothlorian, which worked with mentally troubled people. Among her best-known books are *The Catholic Thing* (1980), *The Passionate God* (1981), *The Re-Creation of Eve* (1985), and *Song in a Strange Land* (1990). She has a cottage in England where she spends time each year writing, gardening, and enjoying family visits — with her ten children and several foster children, now grown with families of their own including twenty-six grandchildren and one great-grandchild.

I remember an evening some years ago that I spent listening to, and trying inadequately to comfort, a woman whose former deep faith seemed to be dissolving into mist. It was happening because what had been most solid — the central figure of Christianity, the Savior, the Healer, the revealed Presence of the Godhead — was itself suddenly evaporating, no more than a construct of a male church, an illusion created to keep women shut up in a system that degraded them by offering delusive comfort and false promises.

The beloved Christ — formerly friend, comforter, refuge — appeared now to be a traitor. A traitor is one whose love and loyalty have been trusted and who turns out to be not only no longer loving or trustworthy but someone who never was, who attracted trust by presenting a false face. This Christ is one who was invited into the secret and inviolate places of the heart who then handed over the keys to the tyrant — the huge, highly organized, patriarchal sys- tem whose very existence depends upon its ability to keep its own feminine side — and therefore women — controlled and subject. This sense of betrayal, of an outrage as deep as that of a woman whose apparently loving husband forces her into prostitution for his own gain, seemed to make any kind of Christian faith impossible.

This is an experience that has come to many women, and it is so painful, productive of such rage and misery, that the only way forward often seems to be to discard the whole Christian heritage and to look for spiritual meaning — if such meaning seems possi- ble at all — in other religious traditions, often in worship centered on the earth and the great Goddess.

Although the desolate story that evening is not my own story, it seems to me very important for women who have not been through such a crisis as this to recognize what it means, for on the credibility of the figure of the Christ depends the credibility of the churches that created such a figure.

The person of Christ does not come to us directly but is con- veyed to us through preaching, through the guidance of spiritual counselors, through art and ritual, so that our prayer itself is formed by the images created by religion. If it comes to seem that this image is deceptive, driving women to accept a submission that suits the purposes of the church structure, then the church itself can no longer command belief or allegiance.

One of the temptations of Christian women who somehow manage to stay with their church is to bypass this challenge and perhaps to dismiss or even mock the spiritual ways of women who have not been able to find any honesty or reality in a system that they feel has used its Christ to imprison women and keep them childish, guilty, and obedient. This matters, and I shall return to the issue.

Saints: The Great Eccentrics

But if I have to give a short reason for my own ability to keep struggling to make sense of Christianity, I would sum it up in one word: saints.

As a child in England I was, like most other children, curious about spiritual matters and fascinated by glimpses of mystery beyond the tedium of everyday necessities. Growing up in a family without any clear religious opinions, going to church (the Anglican parish church) with my grandmother but never told why, I collected my own scraps of vision and information, like a magpie collecting shiny objects, whether a jewel or a piece of broken crockery, to conceal in its nest. Bits of hymns, candlelight in churches, phrases of prayers: I didn't know what they meant, but I liked them and stored them up secretly.

When I was eight years old, my godmother, an Anglo-Catholic, gave me two volumes of the lives of saints. They were bound in green cloth and illustrated with mediocre black and white drawings of a very conventional kind; each story was written by a different author, so that their style varied a great deal and none was very distinguished, as I realized many years later when (after many family moves in wartime, during which the books were packed away) I found them and read them again. Later still they disappeared for good, and I grieve for them, overpious and didactic though they were.

Those books were a revelation to me. They told of men and women who were unconventional to the point of extreme eccentricity, who even as children disobeyed their parents, ran away from

home, lived in caves! These were rebels, loners, people who lived
secret lives that others didn't understand. Whether it was Saint
Bridget making a little altar in the field with an angel for a playmate,
or Saint Catherine being persecuted by her family but seeing visions
just the same, or Saint Nicholas throwing sacks of gold at night
through the window of three girls threatened with slavery, these
were people who refused to fit in, who didn't do what was expected.
They were extremely varied people, from Saint Dorothea being
martyred (and receiving a heavenly present of roses and apples just
beforehand) to Saint Teresa founding a convent and dancing for her
nuns. What they all had in common was a vision of something that
mattered so much that other people's opinions or reactions were
unimportant.

That vision might appear to each one in a different way and
lead one to embrace martyrdom, another to nurse lepers, another to
become a hermit or lead an army to save France, or simply to be a
cook (with angels in her kitchen to bake the bread when she over-
slept). But each person's vision was a revelation of something — a
purpose, a meaning, a relationship — at each one's heart. If it
demanded of each a different response, that response was essential
if there were to be life, if the person were to be real. The alternative
would have been death — death of the self, the soul, a nothingness.
Of course I didn't think in those terms at the age of eight, or in the
years after that when I read and reread those battered, faded green
books. I just felt that, when I read them, I was in the company of
people who knew what life was about.

In the next years I saved up pocket money and bought more
books about saints, and I also read a book of legends about the
Christ-child, which seemed to belong in the same world. So, in an
odd, roundabout way, I discovered the figure of Jesus as one of, as
well as the source and focus of, that marvelous company.

I was lucky. I learned about Christ not through the church but
through the company of the great eccentrics whom we call saints.
And so when I asked for instruction in the Catholic faith at the age
of sixteen, it was because I believed I might share their secret and
their joy. At sixteen I had no trouble imagining myself as a saint, I

just needed the right credentials, and it seemed the Roman Catholic church could provide those!

The elderly nun who instructed me (she had entered the convent in the reign of Queen Victoria) somehow tuned into my state of mind. She gave me books on doctrine to read, but she also gave me lives of saints, this time written for adults, and books *by* saints, writing full of passion and strange symbolism. There were also books of letters between people in the "saint" category — advice about prayer, about spiritual discipline, and about the strange ways of the Spirit. I suppose I understood less than half of these, and I came back to the lives of the saints with relief and to novels about the Catholic martyrs under Queen Elizabeth, stories that gave me a whole new angle on the times of "Good Queen Bess." But even what I didn't fully understand was important. It was a new world, but it was also a familiar world, the world of those old companions in the green cloth covers. And the Christ I encountered during my course of instruction belonged to that world. He was human, strange, courageous, rebellious, angry, grieving, passionate, partisan.

From Committed Catholic to Critic

I became a Catholic, and so, in my enthusiasm for the company of the saints, I accepted without questioning some very distorted spirituality, for many of the saints I grew to know, especially the women, had been themselves the products of a dualistic system that despised all things physical. Even the word "spirituality," at that time, meant to me something apart from everyday life, but something that could somehow be brought into that life by prayers, practices, penances, by going to church often, by candles, religious rites, and ritual — anything that was other than the "worldly" life I perceived around me. The antimaterial nature of the "spiritual" I took for granted, absorbing it from my reading of those holy lives.

I was too young and too fiercely partisan to recognize that their real sanctity, the vivid love and power, had survived in spite of the crippling spirituality that they accepted, and through which their lives were presented by their biographers. Prominent among these spiritual distortions was the use of the concept of religious obedience to keep women under control, to check their generosity, and to dim their vision. This was evident in many stories, and even then I found it hard to accept that it was right, but I supposed it must be.

Fortunately for me, marriage and a very large family made that particular issue a remote one. As my ten children became old enough to listen to stories, I tried to share my own company of saints with them. I also tried to create in our home the old rituals and customs of faith that I had never known as a child but that seemed to me to be the way to feed imagination and give beauty and power to the definitions of religion. (All this was only partially successful in the short term, but now I see some of my children seeking ways to bring mystery to life in their own children's lives, though they don't perceive faith in the way I did — on the whole, fortunately so.)

Yet, wholehearted and committed Catholic that I was, as I grew older I became more critical. I read history and recognized the development of doctrine as a political development designed to support papal and hierarchical power. By then books were being written that questioned the spirituality that had made dominance possible through the creation of guilt. A generation of theologically aware laypeople was beginning to speak out. Long before Vatican II, the tide of unrest was rising. Then the Council responded to that unrest and a great wave of fresh hope, imagination, and energy broke over the Catholic church.

At that time, the first serious piece of writing I was asked to do (apart from short articles, I had not written anything much) was a contribution to a book called *Objections to Roman Catholicism*, one of a series in which believers critiqued their system, whether it was Judaism, Catholicism, or humanism. The essay I was asked to write was on the subject of "Freedom in the Church" and the fact that it was published at all showed the change that had taken place, for it was a historical and moral study of the *lack* of freedom in Roman Catholicism. It was a success with critics, and it was the beginning of my writing career, but it was also the beginning of a long struggle to make sense of membership in a church with a past — and a present — of the kind I, and others, were describing.

To trace the whole story would take too long (and a lot of it is in books I wrote along the way). At this point in my life (sixty-seven, a grandmother twenty-six times, writer, lecturer, working in an organization that does sheltering for homeless families, plus housing and educational work) there are two areas of thought which I explore to help my own awareness of why Catholicism matters to me, and one more which is (rather surprisingly) connected to it and helps me survive spiritually.

The Roots of Symbol and Ritual

The first area is that of symbol and ritual. One day, some years ago, I was watching a movie set (I think) in Greece, in which there was a scene of people coming out of church on Easter night, led by the Orthodox priest in his glittering robes, all carrying candles, and bearing up the great chant of resurrection. The scene was incidental in the story, but it made me reflect on the deep human need for ritual, and the effects of the lack of genuine, bone-deep ritual in most of Western society. It made me aware that the much-emphasized participation, or what churches usually mean by participation, which is conscious attention to words and meaning, is only a small part of the effect of ritual. Ritual goes much deeper than that, for somehow it matters for the health of the community that the thing be done, even if the officiants are inattentive or corrupt, even if the congregation is ignorant or skeptical. I realized in time that religion — meaning the complex of ritual, patterns of behavior, symbols of belief — is something separate from faith, though obviously the two are interconnected. And religion is embedded in the daily life of a community; it depends on tradition and provides continuity. Therefore, it is always at least a little behind the times!

It dawned on me that it matters a lot that Christianity as a religion has roots wider and deeper than its own history, and is not ultimately dependent on specific doctrine or church structure. The church, as it has developed historically, naturally struggles to control what it means by Christianity because it developed as that kind of power structure, a structure that saw its God-given task as ensuring unity of doctrine through the exercise of hierarchical authority.

It did not question that the structure and the faith were inseparable. But in reality we need religion, and especially ritual, yet we don't need a particular type of power structure to provide it and shape it, though there has to be a structure. The version of theology that the church proclaims may or may not coincide with the symbolic meaning of its ritual.

This is a very encouraging and yet unnerving realization, because the Catholic church, in its Vatican II impulse to search for clarity, consistency, and honesty, has pulled away from the obscurity and ambiguity of older patterns. This was necessary; the old way had become too entangled with a passive and even apathetic kind of religious behavior and had already lost touch with the inner power of its own great symbols. This had to do partly with the movement of population from country to city, and with it a loss of sensitivity to the richness of seasonal rhythms and symbols, plus an overemphasis on reason, so that a twenty-minute mutter punctuated with bells and called "low Mass" became the normal liturgical experience of lay people. So when changes were made after Vatican II, they were necessarily made by conscious decision, but the old roots ran below consciousness, and they were all but severed. It was nobody's fault, but it happened. So Catholics were left with a religious system that was, maybe, more honest and understandable (up to a point) but in many ways comparatively superficial and unsatisfying. We felt that loss even if we couldn't identify it. It takes a long time to grow a religious sense and experience. And this is apart from the constant friction arising from issues of clerical authority and later Vatican attempts to enforce its power along Counter-Reformation lines.

Yet the deeper reality of the ritual symbols is still there, submerged and often almost drowned but able to be rediscovered. People are trying to be aware of, and somehow recover, what was lost. The symbolic sensitivity is there, people shaping their communities and hallowing them and renewing them through common ritual. And the real tradition of holiness is there, of men and women of power, wisdom, and passion who prove that the life is still there and that it is worth our rage and struggle.

This is profoundly important for women, because right-brain awareness — the kind that responds to the symbols, the passion, the ritual, the patterning, the relationships that make up religion — is more natural to women, and women often feel the loss of it more acutely. It matters that women allow themselves to feel the loss and to search for ways to be in touch with what has *not* been lost. Women may also distinguish the deeper, genuinely life-giving symbols from those that have been translated and co-opted into tools of cultural conformity as has happened to marriage, or trivialized into near-magic as in the baptism ritual as it is often presented. The search for genuine religion is very difficult, but it must be rooted in the kind of holiness that does not depend on virtuous behavior but on the fire of the Spirit. Men and women share in the search but, paradoxically, women can have, by virtue of their marginality, a greater degree of inner and outer freedom to pursue the significance of holiness and the reality of religion.

Rediscovering Jesus, Friend of Women

The second area in which I find meaning and hope is to go back to where I began and to rediscover the person of Jesus, called the Christ. It was an important moment for me when I realized that it must have been very difficult for Jesus to be male in a society whose idea of maleness contradicted his deepest values. In a society (like almost any society) in which maleness meant and required dominance, control of lesser beings, competition for position, valuation by financial measure, and in which the image of God was designed to validate and reinforce all this, Jesus treated people of any kind as friends, refused to organize other people's lives for them, taught that it is acceptable to be *less*, depended financially on others, prayed to a God who loved children and flowers and had no time for people in love with authority.

No wonder, then, that he had women friends, to the point of scandalizing both friends and enemies. Women could understand his habit of throwing forgiveness about as if it were as common as water — since to him, and to them, it was. Women could recognize the agony of compassion for the hurt, regardless of the moral and social status of the one who suffered. Women, not surprisingly therefore, were the last at the cross and the first at the tomb. And women, once the preaching of the new Way really got going, were soon relegated to submission and controlled as dangerous. They were far too liable to remind the new Christian patriarchs, at some uncomfortable level of awareness, of those values of Jesus that the male disciples had soon successfully rationalized to fit the requirements of acceptability.

The source of the Christian tradition, then, was a man who was not only comfortable with women (many kindly patriarchs are) but was in revolt against the deepest values of a patriarchal society. And *this* is the Christ who made possible the passion of the saints, even though many (maybe most of them at the conscious level) espoused the structure and creeds of the system that had betrayed him. It is painful, for instance, to read Julian of Norwich struggling with the conflict between the truth of her awareness of a mothering, unwrathful God who condemns none and the beliefs of the church to which she gave her genuine allegiance. That reading helps to remind us of the many men and women, lovers of the God of Jesus, who were never named "saints" and in many cases were outcast or even killed because they could not reconcile the vision with the political reality of the church of their time.

But the paradox we live with is that, betrayed or not, the good news of Jesus Christ can be and is carried by the church. The two are entangled and cannot be altogether separated, though it matters desperately that we distinguish them and live out the former not only for the sake of the latter but for the sake of the world's salvation and our own.

The Ancient Goddess

These two areas of discovery — that of religion/liturgy/symbol and that of the recognition of Christ — help me to recognize the complexity of the situation for Christian women. A third area, which I perceive as connected to these, is somewhat disturbing to many women who are trying so hard to keep sane and faithful in a church sick with patriarchal craziness. This is the revival of interest in the religion of the Goddess. It has attracted many women who, as I said at the beginning, find themselves unable to keep honest in a church that has made even the Savior into a jailer. Many of them seek a spirituality that allows healing of body and mind, healing between humanity and the earth that is its home and its own being, healing between intellect and feeling. The ancient Goddess — the mother, the earth, immanent, compassionate, giver of life, and gateway of death — offers to many a way to begin thinking and feeling that is not oppressive but liberating. It doesn't answer all the questions — on the contrary, it allows for questions to remain unanswered yet not rejected. It affirms the womanly perceptions and offers the possibility of the growth of passion, of community, of holiness. It is, in fact, a religious awareness that has the potential to be a religion.

There is a sense in which it is too easy. The remains that we have of the thousands of years when the Goddess shaped the civilization of what has been called "Old Europe" are all archaeological. There was no writing as we understand writing, only a liturgical script. There is not enough to allow us to know fully what that ancient religion entailed. We only know that it fostered a culture without war for thousands of years, a culture that honored in women the power of the divine to give life, that seemingly did not fear death, that saw divinity experienced in animals, had no particular class structure of dominant individuals, and delighted in beauty in even the most everyday objects. When, eventually, this culture was overrun by armed patriarchal systems, it survived "underground" in mystery religions and later in the figure of Mary, mother of God, the irrepressible symbol of woman. What we know is significant, but it doesn't tell us how the worshipers of the Goddess conducted their daily and political lives, how they settled their conflicts (although clearly not by violence) or brought up their children. We don't even know if their theological awareness crystallized divinity into some such word as "Goddess" or "God." (To call it the Goddess civilization is our way of labeling, to help our own understanding; such a label might have meant nothing to them, or even horrified them!) It is easy, and frequently done, to idealize that far off time and re-create a religion that does not deal with difficult issues, and with the dark side of the human spirit, which patriarchal religion certainly did not invent.

Yet, the Goddess culture can provide an extraordinary source of hope for women who are Christians. What those distant memories show us is that it is actually possible for human beings to live in peace, without competition or struggle for dominance, without centralized authority, and yet with a profound religious sense that permeates all of life. This is what Jesus was preaching, but he had the much more difficult task of evoking faith in such a possibility, in such a God, in a society that had been shaped by opposite values. In this man the passionate power of divinity suffered the fate of those who refuse to live by the rules of the system of dominance, but in dying he carried with him into death all that terrible, potent love that cannot die because it is the very nature of life. In his rising he gave it back to the world that had rejected it — gave it to the women first of all.

That life was given back with a new power because it had overcome its opposite. Its victory is not complete because the world that hated it struggles through the centuries to neutralize the power of the fact and the symbol, to adapt it, confine it, and use it. But it will not be suppressed. It breaks out in the great enduring symbols — of Easter and Christmas, of forgiveness and union, in the sharing of food and the blessing of crops. It breaks out in the patterns of caring, the compassion that transcends division. It breaks out in mystical awareness, in all kinds of holiness. It breaks out in the refusal of men and women to be completely conditioned, entirely enclosed in any system that violates the essential interdependence of all creation.

Reclaiming the Fire of Holiness

For myself as a woman the anger remains, and the grief at the pride and deception that has shamed the great and beautiful city of God's people. But the evil things are not at the heart of what I believe Christianity to be. So I believe in the Christ who died because he could not conform to an evil system, and I believe in the fire of holiness that he shared and passed on and that continues to burn and purify, and I believe in the great Mother, whom Scripture calls Holy Wisdom, creator and inspirer, transcendent and immanent, who was and is the spirit of Jesus and of the saints. I believe in the tradition, which is literally a "handing on" of symbol and custom, insight, courage, and hope, from age to age, from each to each, in speech and touch and silence, after the manner of women.

Finally, I don't want to reject the tradition I grew up in (in both senses), however tainted it may be, however entangled with fear of the body and fear of loss of control. We must not allow the desiccated patriarchs to take from us our heritage of Scripture and tradition. We must not let them claim these treasures and distort them and use them to manipulate.

Some people have turned from Christianity in disgust and sought meaning in other religions, including the Goddess religions. But these grew in other places and out of other cultures, past or present. They can help us and we need them, but they cannot heal our own roots. We need to claim, heal, and then pass on to our children the wisdom that is rooted in our own tradition.

Luther is reputed to have said, "Don't let the Devil have all the good tunes." Women should make sure the clerical patriarchs don't keep their grip on all the good stories. They don't even understand them.

Rosemary Haughton

SECTION TWO

EDUCATORS

"To what should I compare the kingdom of God? It is like yeast that a woman took and mixed in with three measures of flour until all of it was leavened."

Luke 13:20

Chapter 5

MUFFINS ON TUESDAYS

Pamela W. Darling

Pamela W. Darling, Th.D., has spent half a century in the Episcopal church. She has earned degrees in English literature, library science, and church history. She presently pursues her taste for muffins and institutional life as writer and consultant for the Committee on the Status of Women, and as special assistant to Pamela P. Chinnis, the first woman president of the House of Deputies of the General Convention of the Episcopal church. After twenty-plus years in New York City, Pam now lives in Philadelphia. She is the author of *New Wine: The Story of Women Transforming Leadership and Power in the Episcopal Church* (1994).

When I was in high school, my best friend Stefi converted from the Congregational church and was confirmed during the bishop's annual visitation to our Episcopal convent boarding school. As a cradle-Episcopalian, I felt somehow vindicated by her decision but was also disappointed by her lack of interest in the more extreme forms of Anglo-Catholic piety that enchanted me in those days. Stefi seemed content with the regular school services: morning chapel where we took turns singing the alto line of hymns and Sunday choral mass (we really did have splendid music) where we amused ourselves during the sermon by passing notes in code. I, on the other hand, was up before the rising bell every morning for the daily office and Eucharist, joined the Sisters for vespers before dinner if it wasn't my week to help in the kitchen, faithfully copied out ancient devotions in tiny handwriting in a tiny notebook kept in a secret pocket of my blazer, and dreamed of becoming a nun. Stefi wrestled with whether the creeds could be literally true; I read about the Desert Fathers and fantasized a life of exotic asceticism. Stefi argued against church traditions that seemed rigid, pointless, or out of touch; I clutched them around me like fortifications against the storms of adolescence.

College separated us, but we kept in touch. When Stefi married a divorced man, one of the Sisters made unforgiving (and probably unforgivable) remarks about adultery. Stefi has rarely been inside a church since then. When I finished college, I entered an Episcopal convent and spent three-and-a-half years exploring from the inside the dream vocation of my childhood. As it turned out, the vowed religious life did not fit after all, and I became a librarian who sang in church choirs and taught Sunday school. I think Stefi could tolerate this phase more easily than she could comprehend my years as a novice, but we continued to talk past each other about religion.

It is sometimes hard for me to fathom just how and why this friend of my heart and I have spent thirty-five years arguing, offending, and otherwise failing to understand each other about God, religion, the church. The chasm became even wider when I left librarianship, returned to school to do a doctorate in church history, and have since supported myself by working in various capacities as a layperson in the Episcopal church. I think Stefi cannot imagine how I — an apparently intelligent, well-educated, competent professional woman with solid liberal credentials and an appropriately raised feminist consciousness — can continue to be part of an oppressively patriarchal institution with a stunning record for being on the wrong side of practically every movement for enlightenment and social justice throughout history. And I find it hard to answer in terms that are meaningful to her.

I remember a story, probably from the heady days following Vatican II, about a Jesuit who was having serious trouble with others in his community because of his radical views. Asked how he could stay with such a conservative group, he thought for awhile and then said simply, "Muffins on Tuesdays." I think I stay in the church because of muffins on Tuesdays — the regular, reliable, steady, predictable, monotonous, tedious, boring, endless assurance that is the Eucharist, feeding my soul weekly (sometimes daily when I've lived in convenient places), uniting all my fears and hopes with those of a million million others, present, past, and yet to come, in that extraordinary mutual offering that is Christ's communion with us.

Like muffins on Tuesdays, this so-familiar experience of corporate worship is a powerful anchor, holding me within a community that contains many things I don't like at all. But can I ever explain "muffins on Tuesdays" to my friend Stefi, who is both offended that the familiar prayer book of our youth has been modernized and critical of its still predominately masculine language and the world-view and values it implies? Can I, for that matter, even explain to myself how I stay in an institution that routinely trivializes, degrades, and renders invisible all who do not match the patriarchal norm — the straight white upper-class male? It is not quite enough to declare that the Eucharist is a communal act, and that to be nourished by it I must remain connected to the community — the institution — in which that act is celebrated. What then?

Baker-Women

I still have that tiny notebook in which I copied prayers in a youthful effort to discover how to know God. Nothing in it looks terribly profound to me today, but I am struck by one thing, one clue, one special ingredient in my Tuesday muffins: My spiritual life was formed by other women. Sisters of the Western Province of the Community of St. Mary taught me for about seven years, first at Ascension Parish Day School in Sierra Madre, California, and later at Kemper Hall in Kenosha, Wisconsin, where I boarded for my high school years, from 1956 to 1960. They were a small but robust group of intelligent, independent women. Most have died (or left) by now, but in the fifties — in the convent and the church as in American society — everything was vigorous, upbeat, booming with all those babies and their parents making a new life in a world supposedly saved from the evils of war. At Ascension I felt supremely safe and loved, notwithstanding the fact that Sister Judith would periodically interrupt herself to command sharply, "Drop!" and we would all scramble under our desks for bomb drills. The Sisters anchored us to the past, to the secure mystery of "the Church," in the midst of the cascading newness of Southern California's postwar population explosion.

My parents became good friends with the Sisters and often visited the convent next door to the church and school, just a few blocks from our house. They would talk and talk, in a glassed-in porch that served as parlor, while my sisters and I raced around the playground and up and down the long gravel driveway. I still have tiny pebbles in my right knee from head-long tumbles on that driveway. I loved going there. They gave us treats. My naval-officer father had a special dispensation to smoke his pipe in the parlor. Right after my youngest sister was born, he was shipped out to sea again, so Sister Elizabetha went to the hospital to see my mother and inspect the new baby. When told that only fathers were allowed to visit the maternity ward, the story goes, she pulled herself up to her full height (I've always imagined her inflating her habit the way a bird plumps up its feathers) and declared, "I *am* the father." Dumbstruck, the nurses let her in. It was that kind of time and place — a close parish and school community where people actively entered into each other's lives. From my childish perspective, it was the Sisters who set the tone, energetically teaching and riding herd on dozens of lively youngsters while challenging our parents to serious spiritual reflection, laughing their way through the California heat in yards of black serge, living love among us from the heart of their celibate community.

I don't suppose it *was* that way, but that is how I remember it, which is perhaps as real now as whatever was really real then — muffins still warm and steaming from the oven. This image of love and safety, framed by all the trappings of Anglo-Catholic practice, took on larger than life significance when we moved again, as the Navy was always moving us. So when the opportunity came to return to the Sisters' care at a boarding school in Wisconsin, I couldn't get on the train fast enough. There, amidst all the anguish of adolescence, the rote faith from my days in Sister Judith's class became my own, argued out again and again with Stefi and our little group of friends. We called ourselves the Tenth Legion, having bonded till death do us part while studying Caesar's *Gallic Wars*. We all read C. S. Lewis, and I also read Brother Lawrence and Evelyn Underhill. We all sang lustily at school chapel services, and I also crept through the dark morning cloister to recite the divine office with the Sisters.

Rising Batter

Batter rises into muffins because gases of fermentation expand in the heat. Like cooking, the spiritual life is fraught with the potential for disaster, and it's a thin line between a delicious snack and a sodden lump. But most of the Sisters knew pretty well where the line was between healthy devotion and spiritual excess, good muffins and moldy bread. They patiently answered my questions, directed me to good books, and encouraged me not to come to chapel quite so often. Dedicated to Mary, they might have been mawkishly sentimental, but they were not, teaching instead, by example, a brisk, attentive approach to the recitation of the office, a completely focused absorption in the liturgy of the Eucharist, and a no-frills, no-nonsense, just-do-it attitude toward daily prayer and Bible reading. Thus was my spiritual life grounded.

They were also — most of them — intelligent, curious, open-minded about theology and Scripture. In a school notebook from 1956, I have a diagram depicting the sources of the Gospels and notes about early collections of Jesus' sayings that are at least as cogent as the ones I took thirty years later in seminary. I was thirteen then and readily caught Sister Margaret Jane's fascination with the latest in biblical criticism. How were we to know it was controversial? Sister said it was fine to ask intelligent questions about our faith, and it was so. Thus was my theological framework established.

No doubt psychobabblers would enjoy analyzing the intense piety of my Kemper days. Their theories would be as true and not true as my rosy memories of a bustling little church school in California are both unreal and real. The point of all this rummaging around in the past is to discover — if it can be discovered — some historical clues to the mystery of my attachment to the church, lower-case "c" as in "earthly institution." Yes, at baptism I was bound indissolubly into the Church, upper-case — the Body of Christ, the blessed company of all faithful people. But I was also enculturated into a faith tradition that was expressed and passed on to me in a particular, perhaps unusual, form. Nuns in impossibly starched head-gear (which must have given them permanent chin and forehead rashes) challenged us with the latest in theology and science. Lay teachers with tantalizingly unknown pasts drilled us in Shakespeare and encouraged discussion of D. H. Lawrence's "Prussian Officer." And we all prayed together — once a day and twice on Sundays.

It is certainly significant that this total immersion in the progressive Anglo-Catholic milieu of the 1950s was mediated for me almost exclusively by women, the Sisters and laywomen who comprised the adult world of Kemper Hall. There was a male chaplain in residence who celebrated the daily Eucharist, and the Sisters dutifully curtsied to the bishop on his infrequent visits. But there was never any confusion about who was in charge of our world. Mother Mary Ambrose and Miss Anna J. Morse, director of studies, together defined the limits of our universe and ruled all that happened within it, as benign and bemused about their responsibilities as they were firm, even dictatorial, when occasion demanded.

Academically, socially, spiritually, our lives were shaped, nur-tured, and sustained by a motley group of intelligent, competent, quirky religious women. In our formative adolescent years, we were spared most of the women-can't-be-leaders conditioning of the wider culture because our *only* authority figures were women, from Sister Prisca who taught shop under the gym in what used to be a bowling alley to the widowed Mrs. Birmingham, impeccably "North Shore," who saw to our training in etiquette; from Marion and Martha who fed 150 people three meals a day with the help of two or three mentally handicapped young women to Sister Hildegarde who played the organ better than almost everyone I've heard in the decades since. Strong female role models abounded, constantly if unwittingly undermining the patriarchal foundations of traditional catholic Christianity.

Daily Bread

It was in this atmosphere that I grew slowly, steadily, deeply aware of God's presence in my life, mediated through the chanting of the psalms in the early morning light and the wise counsel of an old nun who talked me through a junior-year crisis. It was here that my soul was fed day by day, and no matter how many times I watched the mostly handicapped staff stamp out wafers in the altar bread department off the chapel cloister and even sometimes helped to count and wrap them in pre-cut squares of stiff waxed paper, I always knew that the host placed in my hand at the altar rail had become much more than thin flour gruel quickly seared to embossed crisp whiteness. The reality of God became the implicit foundation of my consciousness, and a kind of dumb certainty about God's personal care made a painful adolescence endurable.

The habits of religious practice formed at Kemper Hall carried me through college and were deepened during the years of my novitiate in the Order of St. Helena in the late sixties. There, as the society around us seemed to unravel, we plunged exuberantly into the challenges of liturgical renewal and theological reform. Again, strong women defined the boundaries of my physical and spiritual life. Long before I recognized the narrow confines of women's "proper place" in traditional parish life, I had stumbled into an expansive realm where women exercised autonomy and authority within the very structures of the church. It was in this female world of intellectual endeavor and religious activity that my conviction of God's love for me and God's claim on my life took shape — all bound up with the external trappings of the institutional church.

All that was a long time ago, yet I stay here still. Some of the muffins, "muffins on Tuesdays," have turned out to be hand grenades in disguise, exploding in my face when I suddenly "hear" the misogynist language or subtext of some hymn I always loved to sing. The few gains women have made in access to the full life and ministry of the church, the few improvements thus far achieved in the language of our liturgy, the beginnings of bringing the perspectives of women's experiences to bear on theology and ethics, on church history and biblical studies, initially serve only to demonstrate the overwhelmingly masculinist bias that infects the traditions of the faith. There are days when I think Stefi is right to question how I can possibly stay. There are days when the whole thing looks unredeemable — and then I remember that redemption is somebody else's responsibility.

For all the profound flaws in the church, it was through this institution that the saving Word of God's grace was transmitted to me. Within this institution, strong women of faith created spaces in which girls and young women were taken seriously as individuals precious in God's sight, personally called to pass on that Good News to those who come after. To stay in the church, for me, is to keep faith with those women. To work within the institution against sexism, racism, economic injustice, heterosexism, and all the other manifestations of sin that distort our common life is both to carry on their ministry and to be faithful to my own inner sense of God's will for me. And besides, I still like the muffins.

Pamela W. Darling

Chapter 6
THE WIND SHIFTS

S. Sue Horner

S. Sue Horner, M.L.S., M.T.S., is currently completing course work for the Ph.D. in religion and American culture at Northwestern University/Garrett-Evangelical Theological Seminary, Evanston, Illinois. During the past seven years she has been adjunct professor, lecturer, and advisor, teaching courses and leading seminars on women's studies and Christian feminism in a variety of settings: colleges and seminaries in the U.S. and Sweden, local churches, denominational conferences, and as an international advisor on evangelical feminism at the World Council of Churches' seventh assembly in Canberra, Australia. She has served as national coordinator of the Evangelical and Ecumenical Women's Caucus and on the editorial board of *Daughters of Sarah*. Sue loves good coffee and the coast of Maine.

I live by the sea in the summertime at the mouth of Quahog Bay in Maine with a clear view of the Atlantic Ocean — provided the fog cooperates. It is an amazing spot. The sea and sky in concert with the sun and moon reveal every shade of blue imaginable. The coastline glitters with ledge comprised of multi-hued stone and mineral and topped off by the ubiquitous pointed fir trees. A feast for the eyes and never the same.

Twenty-one years ago this rocky bit of land was the site of a lobsterman's camp. He was ready to retire, and my husband's father wanted a retreat, especially a place that evoked his homeland of Ireland. Today this is now my place of stability, refuge, and reflection. Different generations, different patterns of living, but still a need for the solace of the sea.

Here I slow down to the rhythm of the tides, high and low, in and out, rough and smooth. The tide is something you can always count on. The tide comes in and laps at the high water mark on the rocks and then recedes, twice a day, every day. Every six hours tide pools appear and disappear, treasures from the sea are carried in or carried out.

One of my favorite things to do is to sit on a rock warmed by the sun and just feel the breeze off the water. Sometimes it is so calm — the water flat and still — and then a breeze starts rippling the surface of the water. There is this odd mixture of constancy and abrupt change. You see it everywhere — the sun, clouds, breeze, water, flowers, birds, insects, the moon and stars. I am still surprised by the living aliveness of nature. It is a marvel.

Nature Abhors a Vacuum

Many years ago I attended an exhibit at the Museum of Modern Art in New York City and saw a painting by Helen Frankenthaler entitled "Nature Abhors a Vacuum." This was during one of the first years I spent the entire summer in Maine. I remember the jolt of recognition as I read the title. My recollection of the painting is vague, but I do remember splashes of vibrant colors and the feeling of happiness — a cheerful glimpse of nature. But it is the title that resonates in my mind — a simple yet profound truth. It is my experience, here on the rockbound coast of Maine, that not only does Nature abhor a vacuum but so does God. God's creativity and presence is so apparent here.

But what does all of this have to do with my relationship to the church? The natural world is a spiritual milieu, and these days I'm appreciating even more how attributes of the natural world are equally present in the church, the abiding place of God. Indeed, the church bears all the versatility of God's creation — the good with the bad but always filling all the spiritual holes and cracks.

The church for me has always been this embodied experience of God. Church, of course, understood in these terms reaches beyond physical buildings and Sunday morning ritual. Personally, some of my keenest experiences of the Spirit of God were not felt within the confines of the traditional evangelical Protestant church. Still, it was the practices of the traditional church — Sunday school, Sunday morning worship, Sunday evening evangelistic services, midweek prayer meetings, daily vacation Bible school, sword drills, Bible memory clubs — all of these that have given me not only a strong and abiding sense of God's existence and reality but also an awareness of my own significance as a child of God. This may seem an odd statement from someone who grew up in American fundamentalism. For the typical message one associates with fundamentalism is one of negativity — you are not okay, you are an unworthy sinner. This, however, was not the primary message I heard and definitely not the core of my faith experience.

I grew up in a family steeped in evangelicalism of the Billy Graham variety. Both my mother and father had, as they describe it, "nominal Christian" backgrounds — Presbyterian and Methodist, respectively. Converted after they were married, they wholeheartedly embraced the social mores and theology of evangelicals/ fundamentalists, finding church homes primarily with the Conservative Baptists.

My memories of these churches are positive. Evangelism and saving the world were emphasized more than personal guilt, "feeling like a worm." I will admit though that the primary motivation for my conversion experience, which came when I was thirteen years old, was the desire not to die in an automobile accident and burn forever in hell. (Yes, that was one of several alternatives preceding the altar call each night at a week-long evangelistic meeting at our church.)

In spite of my dubious reasons for wanting to follow Jesus, what stands out so clearly in my mind are the ideas that I am someone very special in God's eyes, that I am deeply loved by God regardless of my behavior, and that God has a specific task for me to do in this world. I knew I was a sinner, but I also knew that if I asked, I would be completely forgiven. I incorporated the forgiven status and the vocational directive. I saw myself as strong — my life verse was Philippians 4:13: "I can do all things through [Christ] who strengthens me." Consequently it also never occurred to me that women might be inferior or secondary to men in the church. Of course, there were no women ministers in these churches, but as I remember it, there was a lot of female presence. I remember women who were primarily active in education and music ministries, but I also remember the missionaries who gave stirring testimonies of conversion and struggle in foreign cultures. Apparently there were sufficient female role models coupled with an abundance of evangelistic imperatives that what I heard and responded to was an active and powerful message — an empowering calling. I truly loved the church and found it to be my home — a place of acceptance and challenge to serve Christ in the world.

All I Was Meant to Be

My feminist journey, at least my conscious journey, began after I was married. That was in 1969. Up to that point my central issues were to proclaim truth (the gospel message as articulated by evangelicals) and champion the underdog (following the example of Jesus). Though not a political person — separatism was the model I grew up with — I had great passion for social justice issues and was particularly impassioned in my arguments against racism. My activism, however, was limited to verbal debate; even though I was in college during the height of the civil rights and anti-Vietnam War movements, I never attended a rally or march, didn't go to Woodstock, didn't smoke (let alone inhale) marijuana, and didn't know what to think of the emerging feminists — "women's libbers" and "bra burners" according to the media. My world was defined by conservative evangelicalism, which in the late 1960s functioned primarily from a separatist, nonpolitical posture.

Some things happened, however, in the early 1970s that awakened the latent feminism within me. First, I got married and had children. Second, and perhaps more powerfully, I began attending my husband's family's church — a Plymouth Brethren gathering.

Marriage and children brought some challenges to my independent ways as traditional female expectations came raining down on me. But it was the church that assaulted my internal instincts about rightness and fairness. Women were clearly second-class citizens among the Brethren. They were not allowed to speak in the "spontaneous" eucharistic worship service (the Breaking of Bread), to teach (except children), to preach (women, especially missionaries, could bring a word or testimony but never exhort). I chafed under the new rules and the humiliation of being designated inferior — subject to men in all things.

At first I responded as a good Baptist — ignore what you don't like or leave. I really did both. I ignored some of the teaching by continuing to view myself as a Baptist. I "left" by serving in the nursery and making coffee during the Breaking of Bread. But the social expectations were wearing me down and my psychic and spiritual salvation only came when we left the Brethren. A difficult time for my husband — these are his roots — and a rejuvenating and healing time for me. I was dying spiritually in that place. This transition occurred when we moved from Massachusetts to California, so in many ways it was less traumatic on our marriage and his family than it might have been.

The California years provided the space and the relationships that helped me identify myself as a biblical feminist. After six years of being told that my innate sense of equality and fairness for women was not a Christian perspective, I was in many ways reborn through relationships with women at an Evangelical Covenant church. But most importantly, my spirit and soul were transformed through the reading of *All We're Meant to Be,* by Letha Dawson Scanzoni and Nancy A. Hardesty,[1] and by attending the 1978 Evangelical Women's Caucus[2] conference held in Pasadena and co-sponsored by Fuller Seminary.

The words of that book empowered me to speak and really begin to use *my* voice. Not only did Hardesty and Scanzoni take the Bible seriously, but they also showed me the embeddedness of male bias in biblical interpretation. As I began to devour books on women in the Bible and women in church history, the enormity and pervasiveness of the view that women are inferior to men — morally, intellectually, psychologically — and that women are essentially untrustworthy, really almost genetically predisposed to evil, challenged me not only to learn all I could but also to work to change these attitudes. I also realized that I had always intuitively trusted my experience as a woman and had made my way up to this point by ignoring "traditional" expectations as much as I could. I remember telling friends, "*All We're Meant to Be* put into words ideas I have been thinking about for years." As I recall this time in my life today, I can say with certainty that it was a moment of epiphany: God's voice called forth my own.

"Grow Where You Are Planted"

Fifteen years have passed since those formative times in the late 1970s. I've raised two feminist children, a son and daughter, am still married to a man who is my best friend and biggest encourager, am still composing a career, and am still in the church.

But, to be candid, these days my church involvement, at least defined as *local* church activity, is marginal. My historic pattern has been to be totally immersed in some aspect of church life, usually in education ministries and social or discipleship programs. In the past five years, due in part to frequency of travel, I have slipped more and more to the edges of ecclesial life and find my involvement in the life of one church is not a priority right now. Instead my passion for God and justice for women has shifted to speaking and being present in a wider arena of churches and national and international church gatherings.

Today my real "home" church is made up of the people who give me nourishment and challenge — most often my Christian feminist women friends. These women do not all live in the same place, so my sense of church is very different from my past thirty-odd years of church life.

Part of this change may have to do with the stirrings of middle age as well as personal growth in things theological. I've recently spent three years doing academic study in theology and am embarking on another three years of scholarly pursuit. This kind of intense focus does shake things up a bit.

The winds have shifted in the fourth decade of my life, and I do not experience these changes as loss but as an enrichment of my experience of God and my understanding of church. Just as the winds shift and the tide ebbs and flows, so too does the journey of faith.

To be clear, I am still in the church. I currently belong to an Evangelical Covenant church in Chicago, though I would not call myself an active member. Neither theology nor community are hindrances to my full participation since it is a progressive and relatively inclusive gathering. Instead it is my moment of distancing and reflection that keeps me on the margins.

For example, recently I spent six months teaching in Sweden. There were many opportunities to travel, and I found myself receiving the Eucharist from many hands, some welcoming to women, others hesitant: my friend Inga in a Mission Covenant church in Sweden; a male cleric in Notre Dame on All Saints' Eve; and a priest in the Athens Greek Orthodox Cathedral (Mitropoli) (it was not the Eucharist but blessed bread). Additionally, this spring I worshiped in a Presbyterian church in Seoul one Sunday, and the next I was part of an African American service in Chicago. The common thread, of course, is Christianity, but my travels reinforce the fact that the expressions and rituals of faith are tightly tied to culture and historical traditions.

I have not given up on the church and certainly have not given up on God. It is really quite amazing how well Christians from Stockholm to Seoul to Sydney to Johannesburg do get along, given the huge differences in cultural practice and theology. However, small steps must increase in number and stride. I firmly believe the church is in need of renewal, and particularly with regard to language, liturgy, and lethargy on all issues pertaining to women. And, I also firmly believe that if enough women raise their voices in their own way and in their own place, changes will occur. Just as a sultry morning in Maine changes to a lovely day when the breeze off the water begins to blow, so too the wind of the Spirit of God blowing through the lives and witness of God's people can renew the church.

Virginia Ramey Mollenkott, a woman I deeply admire and consider a mentor, was once asked how one decides what issue to tackle when the problems of the world and church seem so overwhelming in number. Her advice was, "Grow where you are planted." A simple, yet profound statement like "Nature abhors a vacuum." The answer to why I'm in the church is that I'm growing where I was planted. And, as my work takes me in ever-expanding circles of peoples and places, the message of God's love and justice never ceases to be Good News. I am a Christian and I remain in the church because God is always with me, blowing both her breezes and her gales.

Chapter 7
HOMECOMING

Joyce Quiring Erickson

Joyce Quiring Erickson, Ph.D., is professor of English and director of freshman year and faculty advising at Seattle Pacific University. She has been a teacher and administrator in higher education for twenty-five years, with academic interests in nineteenth-century English novel, women in literature, and women's studies and theology. She has published articles in academic and popular journals on all those topics. She is grateful that her vocation nourishes her avocation — reading contemporary fiction and reviews of contemporary issues. As an active member of her local Presbyterian church and presbytery, she contributes especially in the areas of worship and liturgy. Joyce takes great pleasure in preparing her home and the menu for dinner parties where guests sit at the table long into the night talking about things that matter.

*L*ast fall I walked under a huge tree in the park near my home in Seattle and picked up glossy mahogany horse chestnuts with their powdery caps. I cradled them in my hands as I had done my first fall in Seattle more than thirty years earlier as a college student. I climbed the hill toward home and just as I reached the top, I caught my breath for the hundredth time in months: The mountains were out. It may not be what Wordsworth meant when he used the term "surprised by joy," but it described perfectly my response to touching objects I had forgotten, to seeing blue shadows on peaks that calendar pictures could never imitate, to smelling the alder smoke of salmon bakes on the waterfront. In the evening, as I walked around the lake near my home, the grey overcast of the Pacific Northwest did not dampen that joy. The pewter sheen of the lake's still water, the trill of the red-winged blackbird perched on the cattails by the lake's side, the bluish-green of fir and hemlock on the adjacent hill — to all of these my heart shouted, "Hello. I'm back. I'm home. You're mine."

After more than a decade, we had moved back to Seattle, and now I knew in a sense more profound than ever before what coming home can mean. I'd lived happily in many places in the United States, made many friends who are dear to me still, enjoyed learning the traditions and rituals that make a region uniquely itself, and imagined myself living in many places through which I traveled. In my childhood, my family had moved from Montana to Nebraska to Oregon. As an adult I therefore assumed that moving long distances was an ordinary experience, which my husband, who had lived in the city where he was born until we were married, did not. Whenever I moved, I looked forward to the discovery of new places and new people, and I had never been disappointed.

So during the first months of my return to Seattle, I was not expecting the euphoria that surrounded me like the ubiquitous mist of the Pacific Northwest — gentle and luxuriant nourishment to the roots of growing things. Often I would whisper to myself lines from a Navajo prayer I had memorized: "I walk in beauty. Beauty before me. Beauty behind me. Beauty below me. Beauty above me. It is finished in Beauty." I reveled in the connection between place and spirit — Holy Spirit — that this prayer breathes. And as I read loving descriptions of landscapes in novels or watched the camera's lingering pan over the lights and shadows of water and trees, I recognized, re-cognized, the artists' connection to place that nourished them as the umbilical cord nourishes a wombed child. Like that cord, it also fed them the life-giving liquid of their self, their identity.

It wasn't just the mountains and the trees and the water that compelled me, though. I was entranced by the human presence in this place: the downtown skyline as the ferry pulled into the dock; the way the settlers of the last century had built houses of all architectural styles so close to each other; espresso stands outside supermarkets and auto repair shops. I was charmed by the jostling but friendly and diverse crowds on the urban streets: tall Scandinavian men wearing pony tails and standard business suits; Japanese grandmothers carrying bags filled with produce from the public market; African American college students wearing kinte cloth hats; middle-aged white women on bicycles. This place, like all places we call home, was peopled, and those people had put their impress on the landscape, for better and for worse.

For better and for worse: I was also troubled by the disappearance of woods and fields that had made way for "country living" subdivisions. I was dismayed by traffic rivaling that of Los Angeles and East Coast cities. I was disconcerted by homeless people whose shopping carts and cardboard signs were as familiar here as in other American cities. I was saddened by daily reports of teenage gangs in the south end where the lively prosperity of the downtown streets had not spread.

Home is not paradise. It is what humans have created out of materials they have been given by the Creator, and like all human creations, it is both marvelous and flawed.

• • •

The experience of coming home helped me to understand why I could not ever give up the church. It has helped me to realize that what the church means to me is very much like what my home means to me. Like home, church is not perfect. The institution we humans have made of something we have been given by the Redeemer is flawed. And it is marvelous.

I understood this when I came back to a particular church in Seattle, to the church where the angle of light from the windows was the same as it had been when I was one of the first group of women to be ordained there as an elder. The angle of light was the same when my two sons, now grown, had been baptized. The people who had laid hands on me during the ordination and the people who had vowed to nurture my sons at baptism were greyer and plumper but still there, carrying out those vows for different children, some of whom had been born to people I had known as children.

Maybe we have to leave home to fully comprehend how irreplaceable home is. Though I have never left "the Church," when we moved away from Seattle, I admit I was glad to leave that particular church where trouble was brewing between pastor and people. Since my sons were moving with me, leaving the church where they were baptized mattered not at all. I was more apt to dwell on less pleasant memories, memories like the loss through divorce of dear friends whom we had met in the church. The angle of light from the windows that entranced me when I returned was also there on the Sunday that the hymns choked in my throat, the Sunday after I had read Mary Daly's *Beyond God the Father*.[1] Every trenchant criticism she had made in that book about the church's patriarchy had seemed confirmed in the worship service that morning. So there have been times when I have felt that a particular church, even "the Church," is *not* home to me. And I know my experience of alienation is trivial compared to the suffering and pain many other women have undergone because of the church.

But thinking about the way home is like church has helped me to understand why I cannot choose to give up either. The church will be with me; it has formed me without my choosing, just as my identity is inextricably connected to the places and people of home. You don't choose your home. Your home "chooses" you. And for me the church is confirmation that I did not choose God but that God chose me.

• • •

How does that happen? For me, it began at my childhood home where we knelt for evening devotions with our heads toward the backs of straight wooden chairs. Each of us, children and adults, prayed aloud, and there was no question in my mind that we were praying to Someone who heard and listened. The questions came later as a teenager, some of which I did not dare to ask in my Conservative Baptist home. Did the theory of evolution, which seemed to me eminently sensible, require giving up trust in the Bible, which in my home and church was tantamount to giving up faith? My biology teacher, not in response to a question I asked but in the prescience that all superb teachers possess, explained carefully when we came to the topic of evolution that it was another version of the story of human origins. She said she was a Christian who found no conflict between her faith and trust in the Bible and in the material she taught in school. (Could a public high school teacher talk like that today in the heated atmosphere of controversy over Creationism?) I remember she also said she was a Presbyterian; to my parents that would hardly qualify her as a Christian, at best only what evangelicals of the time called a "nominal Christian," but to me her words were comforting. Thank you, wherever you are, Miss Henderson, for helping me to remain in the church.

It was in a Presbyterian church several years later that the emotional ties to faith and to the church were revived. It's not that I had not been a faithful participant in church life. In fact, my husband was studying for the ministry in an evangelical seminary. For various reasons, we began to attend the large "mainline" Presbyterian church in town, where the worship service included a prayer of confession and other liturgical responses, traditional organ and choral music, and preaching that took the Scriptures so seriously that I learned a new definition for "Bible-based" preaching. For the first time in my life, I looked forward to attending worship because my thirsty soul was watered and my hungry heart was fed. Ironically, for the first time I understood that when my parents said they looked forward to going to church, they weren't faking it. I imagined that their experience must be similar to what I was experiencing for the first time. So though I seemed far from the expression of faith that characterized my childhood home, I was closer emotionally than I had ever been.

Several years later I became a Presbyterian. At that time I was also teaching in an evangelical college, and for the sake of my students as much as for myself, I sought explanations of the scriptural passages that seemed to deny women equality and personhood. I became part of Evangelical Women's Caucus, where I met and became friends with many women from a great variety of denominational backgrounds. Worshiping with these women brought me back to the tradition in which I had grown up (though many from that tradition repudiated them!). They took the Bible and personal prayer as seriously as my father and mother ever had, yet they spoke prophetically about social justice, not just for women but for all the oppressed. The first time I received Communion from the hands of a woman was at an Evangelical Women's Caucus conference. I didn't know how much it mattered until I experienced it. By that time, I'd already read Mary Daly and others who were giving up or had given up on the church. It was my sisters in Evangelical Women's Caucus who showed me a way to stay.

• • •

Since then I've read many other feminist theologians whose interpretations of the faith sustain me. I've been affiliated with colleges whose roots are in the holiness and Roman Catholic traditions. In worshiping with my colleagues at both of those institutions, I discovered additional dimensions of God's infinite variety and capacity to reach us and to connect us to Godself and to each other. These folks were family, and though our dialects were different, we spoke the same language.

That connectedness to the divine and the human becomes clearest to me through words — individual words and words strung together in phrases and sentences. They reach me and touch me like the names of places I've been or streets I've lived on, words like *Kyrie* and *Greenwood*, phrases like *steadfast love* and *Whidbey Island*, words that give pleasure in rolling off the tongue like *Puyallup* and *Ballard* or *Isaiah* and *Alleluia*. When we first hear or say words like these — the words that name places of the earth or of the heart, they have a public meaning and communal function; over time through hearing and using them, they intertwine with the ordinary and extraordinary events of our lives. They become personal as well as communal, connecting us to those with whom we share them, not only people we see and know but people from the past and people in the future. When I encounter these words in unexpected places, maybe at a concert or in an overheard conversation, I experience a *frisson* of recognition and sense of belonging to something greater than my own history. But I also sense that these words belong to me.

I experience another sense of belonging that strikes me as analogous to my sense of belonging in the church when I drive through other neighborhoods in my home city. The contours and landmarks of these neighborhoods are familiar; when I drive through them after having been gone for a long time, they are also reassuring. Even though I don't live in that neighborhood, I can imagine what it's like to live there. That's what I experience when I worship in churches of traditions different than mine. Why do they live in this neighborhood and not in mine? Why their tradition and not mine? If asked, we can give an accounting of the steps that led to our living in a place: We grew up here, or we had friends who lived here, or we came upon the place because someone we trusted recommended it, or . . . it just happened. But that accounting can never explain why it's become home, just as my account of how I belong to the church is only an inadequate sketch of the complicated ways of providence.

Of course, I know there are words that exclude, that shut people out. Women in the church who care about words know this in their bones. But it is those who care about words who can also care *for* them and who can work to give them veracity and use them as faithful representations of experience. Of course, there are neighborhoods that deliberately exclude people through implicit or explicit means. You can either move out of the neighborhood or make it possible for others to move in.

Of course, there are homes that harm and hurt people. For some, leaving home may be the only way to survive or flourish. Or some may be called to leave home for the sake of others they are serving. I think of Simone Weil, one who loved God but refused to be baptized so that she could stand with those who were outside.

•••

There are many aspects of our birth home that we may not cherish or that we may wish to forget. Yet we are inextricably bound to the others in that home by a shared history and by the language and places that have become markers in that history. To those others we owe debts and they to us. So we cannot undo the links that connect us even when we are far away. And when we go back to that home, whether to a place or to the people of our childhood, the smells and the sounds and the objects bring a rush of memories: the blue milk pitcher, the unmistakable lilt of a mother's "hello" on the phone, the smell of the hall closet. And when we sit down to the table, even though we've learned to eat many exotic and wonderful things, the taste of that familiar food is comfort and joy.

And when we sit at table with those who come from east and west, the bread and wine of the Eucharist are like that. The ultimate comfort food, linking us to the past and to the future, when together we will all eat pita and tortillas and chapatis and loaves of dark rye and crusty baguettes.

I know of no other image of the future that stirs me so, an image expressed over and over in passages from the Scriptures like this one from Isaiah:

> On this mountain the LORD of hosts will make for all peoples
> a feast of rich food, a feast of well-aged wines,
> of rich food filled with marrow, of well-aged wines strained clear.
> (Isa. 25:6)

Only in the church can I experience a taste of that future. Only in the church can I work for the coming of that time. Only in the church can I call God to account for God's promises to humankind. Only in the church can I be called to account for my failures to make that image of the future more possible.

The church is home, when I love it and when I hate it. I belong to it, and it belongs to me. And I will stay in this home with all its faults because it is only in the church that I find shadows of the image of the homecoming banquet that God will prepare for all of God's children.

———————————————

Joyce Quiring Erickson

Chapter 8

UNDER THE MANTLE OF MERCY

Janet Ruffing

Janet Ruffing, Ph.D., R.S.M., has been a member of the Sisters of Mercy of the Americas for thirty-one years. A tenured associate professor in spirituality and spiritual direction in the Graduate School of Religion and Religious Education, Fordham University, Bronx, New York, she devotes much of her time to training and supervising spiritual directors. Her book, *Uncovering Stories of Faith: Spiritual Direction and Narrative,* was published in 1989. Janet writes often for a wide variety of periodicals such as *Horizons, Human Development,* and *Studia Mystica.*

I was a latecomer to the women's movement, consciously identifying myself as a feminist in 1978. When I could finally apply what an essay in *Ms.* magazine later called the "F" word to myself, I had just been profoundly disillusioned by my religious community. They had denied my request to begin doctoral studies that year in Christian spirituality. I felt advanced studies and the ministry to which that would lead was clearly a development of my vocation to religious life. As I struggled with this severe challenge to my sense of vocation as a Sister of Mercy, my pain became both more bearable and more meaningful when a Jesuit retreat director that summer suggested that my experience was both entirely personal and also a particular version of oppression experienced by innumerable women. The irony of this situation for me was that this experience of sexism in a religious context was largely the result of internalized sexism expressed against a woman by other women while a male priest illuminated my particular experience of oppression with feminist insight.

This event set the stage for my journey to the present day. Neither men nor women are either entirely enemy or entirely friend. At times feminist men were more helpful to me than the sometimes "animus ridden" quality of some women's groups. And sometimes I found a nurturing sisterhood.

Since I am a Roman Catholic woman who entered a religious order at the age of eighteen after twelve years in Catholic schools, both my experiences of oppression as a woman and incredible experiences of liberating grace have occurred within the same church. Experiences of overwhelming grace, responsible freedom, release of gifts in ministry, and a pervasive sense of divine intimacy have ironically been mediated by the same faith community as have the experiences of exclusion, rejection, devaluation, and patriarchal control. It is the perdurance of these gifts of grace that is most compelling in my choice to continue the struggle, to act intelligently and passionately for conversion of hearts and institutional change, and to recover the "dangerous" memories of the Christian community, especially of the women around Jesus, and of women disciples throughout history.

Moves and Countermoves

On this journey the ironic and paradoxical elements weave their way through the absurd, the ridiculous, and the sad. In the summer of 1978, many Catholic women felt hopeful and expectant of changes favorable to them. Pope Paul VI, who implemented much of Vatican II, was still alive; many theologians expected that their criticism of *Inter Signores* (the Roman document that invented the argument that one had to be a male to represent Christ) would be accepted and that ordination of women might happen relatively soon. Other Christian denominations had ordained their first women. I had experienced a year of feminist awakening, had heard women preach and seen them preside. I had tasted what an inclusive community of men and women might be like. I could imagine myself in the middle of it all both ministerially and intellectually.

Within two years, John Paul II was the new pope. He was so incognizant of the intensity of North American women's pain over their exclusion from ordination that Sr. Theresa Kane, R.S.M., in a prophetic moment, briefly pleaded in public with him to listen to their growing anguish. In her role as president of the Leadership Conference of Women Religious, she "spoke the truth in love" to him in her formal welcome at a gathering for women religious after all efforts to arrange a more informal interview between the new pope and women religious had failed. We viewed his shocked and displeased reaction on television screens across the nation. Women nationwide either applauded or deplored Theresa's actions. I had never felt prouder to be identified as a Sister of Mercy.

Significantly, during that same period of time, Rosemary Radford Ruether gave a public lecture in Southern California where I was teaching high school. I am among the second generation of feminist theologians. My journey has been easier because of the "point women" who preceded me and who taught me. In that lecture Dr. Ruether constructed an argument in favor of women's ordination on the basis of a historical parallel to the slavery question. She outlined two arguments that night which I have never forgotten. One was that the church had accepted the institution of slavery for nineteen centuries and only in the mid-sixties of *this* century, without apology or retraction, simply began teaching that slavery was wrong. She expected something similar would happen eventually with the women's question. Secondly, she argued from history, that leaving a church never changed the group one left. The sectarian option may create something new, but it doesn't bring reform in the original tradition. Inside I felt a quiet but strong resolve. If I wanted the church to change — and I did — I would need to stay in it in some creative and prophetic way.

If I had had any doubts about whether sexism was alive and well in ecclesial practice, there was not so much as a shadow of a doubt by the spring of 1979. When permission for graduate studies was denied, I had been asked to chair the religion department at one of the diocesan secondary schools. The principal was a layman, an able administrator, and good to work with.

In the spring of my first year there, I was dismayed by the announcement that the priest superintendent of schools wanted to give my job to a priest he wanted to attract to the diocese. There was, of course, nothing personal in this. He simply wanted to offer at least a department chair to this man. I was supposed to disappear quietly despite my experience and theological education. This fact was communicated to me by my principal who suggested it might be God's way of helping me get to graduate school faster. I was incensed, to say the least, and refused to agree. Acquiescence for the sake of personal gain was abhorrent. No woman should be treated this way!

The entire story need not be recounted here, but this episode proved to be an important learning experience. For the first time, I realized that my status as a sister did not protect me from gender discrimination. Because I belonged to a community, however, I discovered I did have a measure of leverage that other women didn't have. My religious congregation was now entirely supportive since they understood that what happened to me could happen to any of us. This common threat to female well-being began to heal the rift created by our original conflict. I also received considerable support from other clergy in the area who were willing to support me should a grievance process become necessary. Once again, ironically, a male mentor, my father this time, coached me through the moves and countermoves that eventually helped me keep the chair with three new priests happily joining the department.

Despite the fact that I successfully "won" this skirmish with gender discrimination, I felt disheartened and vulnerable rather than strong after it was over. Every woman who has been in a similar situation knows it can happen again at any time with a different outcome. There is no such thing as really "winning" where there are no recognized limits on clergy power within their sphere of activity.

A Strange and Wonderful Feminist Journey

Due to my persistence and their changing understandings, the leadership of my community reversed its decision and approved doctoral study for the fall of 1980. I gave the first feminist talk in my community in the summer of that year. Although I avoided feminist jargon, the message was clearly a feminist one as I began to raise the women's question against the background of our founder Catherine McAuley's special concern for poor women. That was the beginning of a strange and wonderful feminist journey within my community, which now experiments with a feminine style of governance, provides a feminist support network, uses inclusive language in ritual and public prayer, and is one of those nourishing places in the church where I and other women are flourishing. This concern for poor women has also led among other things to an intercommunity ministry, called Mercy Housing, Inc., which finances, builds, and administrates low-cost housing largely for women-headed households.

This experience with my own religious community, although often more implicitly than explicitly feminist, gives me great hope. As I began to heal my negative experiences with women, I also began to understand how deeply every woman is wounded in her sense of her self as a woman. All of us have learned to devalue or even reject aspects of our femininity as a result of growing up in patriarchy. If we as a community of women have begun to heal the wounded feminine in us, to honor our reality, to celebrate our gifts, even as we turn toward the world in compassion and care, perhaps, in time, a similar transformation will occur in the larger body of believers.

Such communities of women and sometimes men are church, too. The more I allow myself to believe that the more I am sustained in this journey.

Because of the very real pain in every churched woman's story, once she allows herself to become conscious of it, the choice to continue membership is not easy. Who among us has not debated whether to stay or to leave in the midst of some public liturgies when attempts to worship with the gathered community become "near occasions of sin" — those times when anger overwhelms consciousness in spite of years of practice of not listening to antiwoman preaching and to the persistence of sexist language in readings and prayers? We wonder, Why not spare ourselves this frustration? And yet, we stay in the church if not always at such liturgies. Why?

Part way through my doctoral studies, I faced a dilemma. The question I posed was "What kind of theologian am I to become?" I had already become feminist in my critique, but by the early eighties, post-Christian feminism was already a reality. As I sat in prayer, frightened even to have asked such a question, there arose before my inner eye, one by one, the Christian feminist women with whom I had studied. From some place of inner knowing, I understood that my most fundamental experience of God had always been mediated by Jesus and by some part of the community that gathered in his name. Since this was the truth of my life, a post-Christian position would be a betrayal of my core experience of grace. From that time on, my conviction has only deepened. But it has required a deconstruction and reconstruction of more than I could have imagined.

Increasingly, I am convinced that we stay because we exercise so well the "powers of the weak," as author Elizabeth Janeway describes them.[1] We refuse to believe that which suggests we are not ordainable, capable, worthy, graced, or in the image of Christ. More than that, we persist in believing in our call to fullness of life.

The source of this belief lies not so much in the women's movement as it does in the gospel. The secular women's movement has helped us wake up, see, and resist the Christian community's failure to fully embody the gospel in relationship to women. It has

helped us recognize a need for conversion in the direction of inclu-
sion, in the direction of spirit, in the direction of the flourishing of
female humanity. This kind of believing does not come easily. It
requires a revolution in our thinking and a refashioning of our
images of God.

When I began to experience the dissonance between a feminist
reading of the gospel and my internalized patriarchal readings of
those same texts, a battle royal ensued. It was as if I could not let
God, the enforcer of patriarchy die. Somehow, because the image of
God has been so distorted by patriarchy, it creates a crisis of belief
when we reject it. Patriarchy seems to own this god, and its image is
embedded in language, ritual, and practice. Thus it felt subjectively
as if I were rejecting *God*, the real one. In the beginning, I felt guilty,
ambivalent, and helpless, but as I stayed with the contrast through
days of retreat, a deeper experience emerged. I discovered that
despite the seeming solidity of this god who was hostile to my
deepest being, in the end it had to be an idol. Welling up within me
were surprising experiences of tenderness, love, compassion, presence, and above all a quality of courage that felt grounded in truth.
There was new freedom! I began to feel with this kind of God as if I
were standing on a Rock — somehow grounded, strong, supported. I doubt that this would have happened for me without the
support of sensitive feminist spiritual direction — again men and
women who supported the new consciousness.

In the beginning I could not image God in feminine terms.
Patriarchy felt so big, so *male*, that a feminine God-image did not feel
strong enough to me. Living in Berkeley during the early eighties, I
felt there was something wrong with me if I couldn't pray with a
feminine image of God. At that time, I needed a God who could
protect me against the power and system of male control. Yet I
always had to distinguish between the system and the actual men in
my life. In my personal history I have received more masculine
nurturance and mentoring than most people. I have often been
treated more kindly by men than by women. And the world opened
to me by men felt generally larger and more expansive than the
typically female world.

However, in time, and through considerable reading, I came to a new relationship with the feminine itself, which is leading me into two different kinds of experiences with God. Sometimes my images of God remain masculine in their quality and their felt sense. This transformed masculine sense of God, however, is fully accepting of my deepest and often rejected feminine self, something none of the men in my life are completely able to offer. My full power, intensity, and truth is often "too much." When God meets me in this place, I am confident that I am not too much for God — that my being pleasures God, and I return to myself more comfortable with my feminine reality.

I also have feminine images of God that emerge spontaneously in my psyche. I listen to Christian feminist music and find myself deeply nourished by it.[2] It is as if my deepest feminine experiences are literally appearing in vision and finding voice. Since my primary academic discipline is the field of spirituality, I have found Caroline Bynum's historical studies on the way symbols functioned for medieval women extremely helpful.[3] She notes in a number of different studies that symbols cannot simply be "created from thin air." They have their own internal logic. Symbols that may seem unfriendly to women from our twentieth-century point of view were often not at all that way for medieval women. They may have been paradoxically empowered by such images. Likewise, in my own deeper experiences I am often surprised at the way an image may incorporate something I once rejected and present itself in an entirely new and encouraging way.

Mantle of Mercy

Through much of my life I have felt a great deal of ambivalence about the symbol and role of Mary in Catholic tradition. When I was honest with myself, I had to admit some resentment. Mary was presented as the only woman who could simultaneously be both virgin and mother. Her image was so "god-like" it was impossible for me to really identify with her. Gradually, however, I began to see her as an unwed mother, a refugee, the mother of a son executed as a criminal, and a leader among the early community of disciples.

Not long ago, however, I encountered an image of Mary that both surprised and delighted me. At a time when I was feeling the normal pressures of masculine expectations and *modus operandi* of university life, I visited the Metropolitan Museum of Art's Sienese Exhibit. I came upon a Madonna of Mercy — an immense fresco displayed over a doorway. Designed for an entry way to the women's section of a medieval hospital, the image was rendered in a horizontal pattern rather than the vertical one more typical of the figure. This Madonna, holding the Christ, had an extraordinarily wide mantle. In the folds of her mantle on one side were important church people, on the other temporal rulers. In that one image, suddenly every aspect of patriarchy was relativized. This archetypal Great Mother was the necessary gateway for all such male authorities. They were all under her mantle, dependent on her for protection and care. The experience happened in one unified moment of consciousness.

Sometime later, while at prayer, I found myself completely wrapped and protected in that mantle. This great maternal figure was alive for me in an entirely new way. Clearly, this was a God image — an amazing experience of the feminine face of God. And she was certainly powerful enough to shelter me from the threat I was feeling from patriarchal behavior. Sometime later I read an essay on Mary by Elizabeth Johnson that confirmed my sense that this image belonged more to God than to the human Mary.[4]

This latter experience of finding a feminist theological essay that deepened my understanding illustrates yet another hopeful sign for me. There is an increasing correspondence between the experience of women and the theological articulation of reformist feminist theologians. Reading other feminist writers in my tradition confirms many of my own thoughts and feelings. My experiences are clarified when I can find new ways to understand them. As insight develops, my experience changes. There is now a growing body of feminist work in all fields to support this kind of interaction between reflection and experience. No longer are our experiences as women being explained away, ignored, or trivialized.

There is a long interior journey that I have traversed and on which I have accompanied other women in spiritual direction. Like the central character in the play and film *Shirley Valentine*, we wake up, having recognized the unnecessary restrictions within which we have led our lives. And with her, we realize that we are often living very small lives when, in fact, there is so much more to us. If we weren't meant to live larger, more fulfilling lives, we wouldn't have such feelings and dreams and hopes. For me, these dreams, feelings, and hopes are rooted in my experience of a liberating God who does not will our oppression but who suffers with us and who offers us fullness of life in the midst of this struggle.

As I reflect on the current state of gender affairs in United States culture, we seem to be entering a new phase. Although we have a legal framework for ending discrimination, we find that implementing such change affects both men and women in some deep core of the self. As we continue to live courageously into the awareness of a new relationship between the genders, each of us will undergo much more change. Our habits of thought and behavior are deeply engrained. Even when our behavior changes, our attitudes and beliefs do not necessarily follow. And even when our beliefs change, our behavior may take a long time to catch up. Understanding this helps me to be compassionate, to appreciate the depth of the feminist challenge, even as I introduce a whole new group of international students to this challenge, often for the first time, in my teaching each year.

Although change on gender issues at the institutional level in the church has only just begun, Catholic feminist reflection is already entering a creative, constructive phase. Each of us does what we can in teaching, in ministry, in writing to support this movement. I continue to believe that we are involved in a paradigm shift that will not be stopped because it is rooted in compelling truth and because God's gracious Spirit will bring it to completion.

A Consoling Word

Some time ago I was leading a worship service for my community. It was a Communion service at which I had been invited to both preside and preach. Since it was the end of Easter week, the text that morning was Mark's version of Jesus' post-Easter appearances, first to Mary Magdalene, who tried to tell her unbelieving brothers, then to two walking in the country, and then to the eleven (Mark 16:9-20). When I reflected on this story, I was amazed at a twofold movement. The disciples rejected Mary's testimony because their weeping prevented them from hearing or seeing the new life in their midst. In the final scene Jesus appears to the eleven (all men) whom he scolds for not believing the testimony of those who had seen him, and then he commissions them. Against the backdrop of the persistence of male clerical rejection of the testimony of all the Marys among us, I heard a very consoling word that morning. We need to be sure that we are not so busy with our lamenting that we fail to recognize the new and amazing ways in which Jesus brings life out of this anguish. We need to continue to speak our truth courageously, bearing witness to the experience of Jesus that is ours. And we can hope that eventually Jesus will work the necessary conversion of heart in the clergy to once again affirm and incorporate the full discipleship of women in leadership, in proclamation, and in ministry in our own times.

Janet K. Ruffing, RSM

SECTION THREE

STEWARDS

"At that time Deborah, a
prophetess, wife of Lappidoth,
was judging Israel. She used to sit
under the palm of Deborah
between Ramah and Bethel
in the hill country of Ephraim;
and the Israelites came up to her
for judgment."

Judges 4:4-5

Chapter 9

THE RHYTHM OF RENEWAL

Marjory Zoet Bankson

Marjory Zoet Bankson, M.A., is president of Faith at Work, Falls Church, Virginia. Her role in this national leadership development ministry complements her commitments at the ecumenical Church of the Saviour in Washington, D.C. Much in demand as a retreat and conference speaker, Marjory has also recently completed a video of biblical monologues called *Tongues of Fire: Five Women from the Book of Acts*. She has published three books with LuraMedia: *Braided Streams* (1985), *Seasons of Friendship* (1987), and *This Is My Body: Creativity, Clay, and Change* (1993).

*L*osing heart and finding it again has been my path to the presidency of Faith at Work, a national renewal ministry that I've directed for the past nine years. Even here, the heartbeat of hope and despair seems natural to me. We depend heavily on volunteer help and individual contributions that fluctuate continually. Nothing is perfect or permanent. Maybe trusting this rhythm of renewal is a mark of being slightly more than middle-aged because I know that new life comes again — often in a different form than before. This is my resurrection faith.

Language of Prayer

But the doctrines of the church are a different matter. As a woman, I have felt boxed and labeled, my leadership limited by a male hierarchy. Still, the church has been a place where I looked for kindred souls — people who wanted something more from life than power or entertainment. Church music has given me language for my prayers, and biblical stories have stretched my thoughts beyond the here and now. In church it has been all right to talk of God. To listen, too. I grew up loving a place to savor a Presence I could not catch or count.

As an adolescent, I found quiet in an unexpected place — at the mortuary where I practiced the pipe organ because the church was unheated during the week. I was drawn to the mystery of life by being in the presence of dead people every morning before going to my high school classes. They were different from people who were simply sleeping. "The difference must be soul," I thought. "And soul comes from God and goes back to God, like breathing out and breathing in."

Language of the Soul

When I went off to college, I left the church, sure I would learn enough that I would not need the quaint and pious ways my parents seemed so dedicated to. About two months into my freshman year, however, I sneaked back into a mid-week chapel service because I was feeling terribly lonely for a space and quiet to simply sit, to let my anxious thoughts find rest. Not long afterward, I was asked to join the chapel choir, and I gladly helped to fill the sacred space with song, not quite aware how tempting it would always be to fill my yearnings with activity. The church often cooperated with that cultural habit rather than calling me to silence and contemplation.

When my husband went to Vietnam, I went into depression — and found God there, in a pottery studio. In the evenings, after teaching school all day, I began to work with clay in the empty studio of a family friend. He invited me to use his "therapy wheel" when he was finished for the day. I had the time and space to begin over and over again without anyone watching or judging. A place of silence and contemplation was simply given. As I worked with clay, the message of resurrection began to come clearly — nothing is wasted, everything can be remade, life is about learning and letting go.

In church I had learned the language and the stories of Jesus. In the pottery studio those words became grounded in experience: healing, teaching, community, crucifixion, and resurrection. Working with clay, my hands learned to trust the earth and the creativity deep within, to make clear choices and to let go of what I didn't need to save. In a small, contained way, I was learning to live with life and death, to trust the possibility of renewal after something flopped or failed in the firing.

Clay became the language of my soul, a place where body and spirit could meet and meld. Because I didn't fill the silent studio with sound, my mind had space to wonder and observe, to expand beyond the fear that my husband would be killed or taken prisoner, to trust the tradition of handwork I was participating in by making useful pots. I began to believe my own life had meaning beyond being Mrs. B. Now, I would name that experience "God's call." Then, I had no language for what was beginning to emerge — except to watch and take pleasure in the forms my hands were shaping.

Language of Hope

When we moved to Washington, D.C., in 1976, we became part of Church of the Saviour, an ecumenical church with a tradition of conscious commitment to the inward and outward journey. Just one month before we arrived, the original church had divided into six little churches, each with a particular mission focus. We were drawn to Seekers because of its intentional focus on inclusive language, shared leadership, and equipping people to understand their ministry in daily life.

One thing that makes Church of the Saviour different from other churches is that we do not speak of "empowering the laity" but of making all members into ministers. The membership process takes at least two years and involves attending classes, identifying a mission and joining a mission group, becoming accountable to a spiritual director for daily disciplines, attending weekly worship, giving proportionally of time and money, and making regular silent retreats. Membership is an ordination process, of being called by God and confirmed by the community.

By the time I became a member in 1978, I was not only teaching classes but preaching regularly and serving Communion with a male liturgist since we wanted both male and female presence at the altar to embody the whole image of God. In Seekers, efficiency is not the measure of success, nor is bigness a goal. We currently have twenty-two members, and on a typical Sunday we have about seventy-five adults and forty children at worship. The service is "made by hand." Many people participate, coordinated by Celebration Circle, the mission group in charge of worship. Sometimes we cannot contain the variety, and people disagree about the liturgy or the sermon, but we are not afraid to fail. The rhythm of renewal is always there.

Being in this kind of a church gives me hope for the future. At Seekers, I have found a place to grow, to offer my gifts, and to be received as I am. It's the intentional family I believe Jesus collected around the table, doing "the will of God" by being together, breaking social barriers and cultural taboos as he revealed a body-connection his followers had not known before. At Seekers we do the same thing, pushing against the addictive individualism our society holds up as autonomy.

Language of Relationship

During the sixties and seventies, *Faith at Work* magazine introduced me to another group of articulate Christians who were at work in the world. Not clergy or systematic theologians, these people spoke my language — of relational ministry in daily life. In the magazine and at Faith at Work conferences, women and men were free to make connections between the teachings of Jesus and their own work. Since women were not yet visible in church leadership, I found new models for my own sense of call in the Faith at Work network of people and ideas.

My first invitation to lead a church retreat came through a Faith at Work connection in 1976. By then, I had been teaching adults in a local church for three years, using Faith at Work methods and adding art exercises to encourage holistic learning and awareness of relational community. The church was a place where I could offer classes, and the people who attended became my "intentional community" within the larger congregation. I found real joy in leading others to their own discoveries, but my own spiritual growth took place beyond the church, through books, conferences, and reflection on daily life.

In 1980 I was asked by women on the Board of Directors to help design the first Faith at Work event for women only. We decided to balance verbal and nonverbal input, to work with one biblical story instead of many, expect the leadership team to function as an organic whole instead of skillful separates, and provide an extended period for each woman to tell her story in her own way to three other people. "Hearing each other into speech," as Nelle Morton describes in her book, *The Journey Is Home*,[1] has become the centerpoint of these Faith at Work Women's Events. Such a simple format could go far to help the church reclaim its power of healing and communion.

For two years I worked as the volunteer coordinator for the women's ministry of Faith at Work; then I asked to be paid for doing the same thing while I attended Virginia (Episcopal) Seminary. Opportunities for writing and speaking continued to come from different churches and denominations even beyond the Faith at Work network, so I had a chance to verbalize the images and metaphors emerging from my search for God's wholeness and to practice working with different groups as I had once worked with clay.

In 1985 the board of Faith at Work asked me to run the office while they sought a new president. Begun by Sam Shoemaker more than fifty years before, Faith at Work had always been headed by a man, so I wasn't sure they would take my candidacy for the presidency seriously. Knowing also that churches and related ministries do not usually hire the interim person, I hesitated and decided to go on a silent retreat, where I screamed and yelled at God about the injustice of being a woman in the church. Then I listened for God's response. What I heard was "Say Yes, but put a time limit on it. Let your work speak. Ask to be considered as a regular candidate."

So I did and was selected. The time was right for a woman's energy and style. By 1985 what we had learned in the women's ministry could be shared more broadly with a new generation of men and women who were searching for models of partnership. Since then, my focus has been to reclaim and work with the stories of biblical women as a framework for looking at contemporary life.

• • •

It's clear to me that God is at work in the world — in, through, and beyond churches. The Bible is full of stories about ordinary women and men who paid attention to their inner knowing and let the Spirit guide their outward actions on behalf of God's larger purpose. We are no different. Perhaps God's antidote to perfection is our finite lifespan, for each of us must traverse the stages of faith and learn to live with the uneven heartbeat of hope and despair until we die.

From where I stand, this looks like the most exciting time since Jesus walked the earth and welcomed women as full human beings. Although the church closed down those options as it organized and took on the cloak of culture, individual women have courageously spoken their truth and borne witness to God's call for two millennia. Now a critical mass has formed, and women are claiming the place in public leadership that Jesus called us to.

I believe that we may be at a point when renewal of old structures is no longer possible without breakage and re-formation, but God's biblical story is surely a record of death and resurrection of institutions and communities, as well as of individuals. We can trust the rhythm of renewal. For women today, the time is right to claim the larger vision for humanity that Jesus lived in full view of the earliest disciples. It means reshaping the image of God at every level of being, beginning with ourselves and our closest relationships and extending as far as our gifts and vision can take us.

Chapter 10
FOR ME, GOD IS

Laura E. Wright

Laura E. Wright is retired staff officer for stewardship of the national Episcopal church. She has written professional materials on the educational process involved in turning reluctant tippers into grateful tithers. She is a laywoman, native New Yorker, and a lifetime Episcopalian. Laura Edna was educated in New York City public schools and is presently attending the College at Sixty program at Fordham University's Lincoln Center campus. She is immersed in congregational and diocesan leadership activities as well as writing short stories, essays, and memoirs as part of her school work and her participation in the Crescent Street Writers Group.

*I*n my life, there is God. Every moment of my life, for as long as I can remember, there has been God. I have written articles, sermons, and essays about God and me. Yet, when my fourteen-year-old grandson asked, "Why do you believe in God?" I could not answer him in a way that he understood. I could only reply, "I just do!"

He pressed me further. "Grandma, what *is* God?" I hesitated. I thought. These words are important. What I say will mean something to him. He is not a Christian, and he is wondering why I am. Speechless for a long while, I could only reply that God is love. Then came the statement that made me wish I were an eminent theologian. "I think, Grandma," he said, "that people created God, not the other way around. People needed something, anything, to help them through life and its problems, so *they* created God."

What could I say to that, I thought. Why could I not come up with words of wisdom? Where was the great insight needed to address this challenge? Where was the Holy Spirit in my time of need?

I know it was not enough, but all I could say was, "I believe God created." The only thought I had, the only thing that came to mind, was the words of the Creed: "I believe." I was afraid to go further. I only sat there and wished I were someplace else or maybe someone else who could explain to this young man what I felt and knew deep in the very core of my being.

How could I explain that God is not just *in* my life but *is* my life? What could I have said to rationalize that? There is no way. To my grandson, and to many others, that is a totally irrational concept. Somehow I could not tell him that there is no time I can ever remember not believing in God. I have a difficult time understanding that myself sometimes, so how could I explain it to him?

What an important conversation that was for me. It made me look very closely at my relationship with God. Realizing that my faith and my beliefs are so ingrained and intense that I can't articulate them to a person who doesn't believe was so illuminating as to be painful. It even made me question their reality.

Before Remembrance: God

When did my belief begin? Before remembrance. I can't put a date or time or place on it. Sometimes I envy those who have had a conversion experience. I am astounded by people who have had recent religious encounters and can tell the exact time and day that Jesus came into their lives. Folks who can stand up and expound on the difference in the way they lived before and after knowing God are enviable. As for me, I can't remember not believing. I can't remember a day that didn't include prayer. Sometimes brief, often out of habit, but daily prayer. I can't recall a Sunday that I did not expect and plan to be in church. I don't remember being carried there, but I'm sure that I was, long before my memories of toddling between Mama, my sisters, and brother to the Church of the Redeemer, Astoria, New York. Redeemer: Where my parents were married, where I was baptized, and where I worship still.

The Church of the Redeemer was where it all began, but who started the process? Mama. She's the one. It was Mama who was responsible for my "I believe." Not just because she took us with her to church every Sunday. Not because she taught us to pray each day. But because she believed and trusted in God, and showed me and my sisters and brother how to do the same.

Mama was widowed when I was three months old. There was no earthly father, and so the image of God the Father was a good one for me. Trusting in a parental God was easy to do as a child, and it seems to me, looking back, that there were many opportunities to rely on "Our Father, who art in heaven." Perhaps I even confused the two somewhat, the dead earthly father in heaven (according to Mama) and God the Father, also in heaven.

I recall one day in particular when Mama's strong faith became very real to me. My brother George was very ill. He was seven years older than I and always sick. He suffered from rheumatic fever, epilepsy, and unexplained stomach pains of such severity they required morphine to ease the agony. I don't recall exactly what the problem was that day; I only know I wanted to escape from it. So, I went under the dining room table.

It was a good place. No one could see that I was crying. It smelled good under there, too. From the lemon oil. Mama had given me a dust cloth and lemon oil soon after the doctor arrived, and she had provided strict instructions to polish the dining room table legs. There were four of them reaching out from a huge tree-trunk base. They were shaped like bear claws. That made it really difficult to polish them. You had to get the dust out from between all the little toes. Under the dining room table was a good place to be, hiding from all the activity.

Mama was crying, Georgie was moaning, and the doctor was on the phone with someone at the hospital. "What a shame. So young. High fever. Send an ambulance, right away."

His words were so scary. I couldn't bear to see them take my brother away, so I stayed under the table until they all left in the ambulance: Mama, George, and the doctor. I was left home alone. In the quiet. Waiting.

By the time Mama came home, I was out from under the table. She told me it was time for us to get supper ready for my sisters who would soon be home from work. She admired the dining room table legs, told me how helpful I was, and how much she loved me. When I asked about George, she said that he was being taken care of by good doctors and nurses, that we should pray for him, but that right then we had to prepare dinner. "Life goes on," she said. She *always* said that. No matter the troubles and worries, she would say we must trust in God and keep going.

An eight-year-old child is puzzled by that kind of thinking. At least I was. Her advice was *always* to pray, cook, laugh, eat, love, and trust in God. What a strange way to live! But it worked. George didn't die then. He lived fifty more years through similarly anxious days including kidney failure, dialysis, and transplants.

But Mama didn't. She died when I was twenty-one. Some days when I want to go under my dining room table with soft cloth and fragrant lemon oil, I recall Mama's instructions. When I want to be far away from stories of violence, broken promises, bad decisions, and fear of the future, that voice and gentle smile come back with all their love and faith. So I stay on my feet. I remember to trust in God, to pray, cook, laugh, and eat. Under the dining room table is still a good, safe place, but it's not where life goes on.

From Icon to Brother: Jesus

As a child and young adult, I thought of God only in the parental sense, perhaps because my father was dead, or maybe because Jesus seemed separate from my view of who God was. Going to Sunday school and singing in the junior choir gave me a childlike view of God's son that carried well into my adult life. Jesus was a little figure in the creche at Christmas time. Jesus was the naked man hanging on the cross on Good Friday. Jesus was the reason I had a new outfit for Easter.

It wasn't until decades later that my relationship with Jesus changed. I experienced Jesus in an entirely new way as a result of attending a renewal weekend for women in the spring of 1986. The weekend began on a warm Thursday evening in May. My renewal weekend sponsor had driven me from my home to the conference site on Long Island. As he left, my enthusiasm left with him.

I went through the motions the first two days: praying, meditating, studying, singing. Very little was new to me except for some of the music. None of the ideas excited or challenged me. I took part in the activities almost by rote, but deep inside I was bored and restless. I wondered why I had let myself become involved. By late afternoon Saturday I was tired of the whole process and ready to pack up and go home. I had had enough of those crying, laughing, bell-ringing females!

I shared my feelings with one of the leaders, and she encouraged me to "hang in." She suggested that I give myself a little more time. After all, there was only one more day to go. Now I was incensed! Give *me* more time?! There was nothing wrong with me! It was the rest of the group that wasn't up to par as far as I was concerned.

After Saturday night's rather light and festive activities, Sunday finally came. We were awakened before dawn with fragrant, colorful flowers and joyful music. We moved through a warm spring day with morning prayer, well-planned meals, preparations for the closing celebration of the Eucharist in the afternoon, and packing to go home. The leader of the weekend recommended at lunch that we spend part of the early afternoon alone, silently reflecting on our three-day experience. And so I retired to a quiet courtyard and looked out on the grounds where other women were walking, some reading their Bibles, some at prayer, some in pairs talking quietly.

I realized then that I had come to that weekend with unrealistic expectations. I wanted thunder and lightning. I was looking for comforting voices in the night and wondrous miracles by day. Instead I had received tender care from strangers, understanding and forgiveness of my judgmental attitudes. Out of a diverse group of women came a strong community of faithful partners with Christ Jesus. As I looked at them strolling in the warm May sunshine, I saw Jesus in each face as they passed by and smiled lovingly at me.

That afternoon the chapel was standing-room-only as hundreds of people from many congregations in the diocese as well as family and friends of the participants came to celebrate with us. During the service we were each given the opportunity to make a brief statement about our experience. I don't recall everything I said, but I do remember that I compared myself to a pitcher that had spent the past three days being filled up and emptied out. Filled day by day with prayer, study, songs, and laughter, and poured out again in confession, tears, and silent meditation. On Thursday and Friday I had been composed of ceramic: opaque and ready to crack if dropped. By Saturday I had changed into crystal: sparkling, sheer, and primed to shatter into a million pieces at the slightest provocation. But by Sunday, the day of rebirth and resurrection, I was sterling silver. I felt solid, glowing, reflecting light and images. I knew I might be dropped and dented, I might tarnish in days to come, but I could always be polished again and returned to a radiant, open, welcoming vessel, ready for ministry.

That weekend was a new beginning in my relationship with Jesus. No longer was he merely a far away colorful image; he became my beloved companion.

Life Support: Holy Spirit

Very significant changes occurred in my life in 1979. It was a year of turning points. I began my work at the national offices of the Episcopal church, and my husband died.

Many people have asked me how I happened to get my job at the Episcopal Church Center in New York. For a long time I would reply that I responded to a notice of open positions in the Diocese of Long Island's newspaper *Tidings*. That's not really true. That was part of it but not the whole story. I was ashamed to tell how it *really* happened. I was embarrassed. I thought they would laugh at me. Not any more! Now when someone asks, I proudly admit, "It was the Holy Spirit!"

The story began one cold winter day when I arrived at my job at an architectual sign company. I thought I had a good job, a fair salary, and a position where I was appreciated. But life in general was not easy. At the time my husband, Tom, was working for a well-known department store chain and earning less money than I was. Our son was living on his own by then, but our teenage daughter who was ill with anorexia nervosa was still at home. I arrived at work that snowy February morning to find no heat in either the office or the plant. The thermometer on the wall read twenty-three degrees. I was the only person in the office; anyone who had come in before me had gone right home. Because the furnace had gone off, the pipes were frozen and there was no water or toilet facilities.

I called the president of the company, who was still at home, and told him of our predicament. I mentioned that I had already called a plumber and the oil company; both would be on their way shortly. He told me to stay there until everything was in working order and he had arrived. Apologizing for having to "disobey," I told him I would leave and come back only when the building was warm. He hung up.

About noon, my phone rang at home. It was the president of the company, my boss. I asked if everything was all right, and he said it was. Thanking him for calling me, I told him I would be there in twenty minutes. His next words were, "Don't bother. You're fired."

I thought he was joking. He said that anyone who wasn't willing to be inconvenienced somewhat was not welcome to be in his employ.

I couldn't believe it. I had worked as his assistant for four years! He said again that I was finished and that they would mail me my final check. This time I hung up. I was furious! Calling back, I told the receptionist I would be in shortly since I wanted to say goodby to everyone, and I needed to clean out my desk.

It was a painful experience. I marched into my now ex-boss's office and very sarcastically wished him well and shook his hand. "Why?" I asked. His response to my question was the same as it had been on the telephone. A very puzzled and dejected woman drove home that frigid February afternoon.

A few days later I received a check from the company for my portion of the profit-sharing plan. After five years' employment, I would have been fully vested, and they would have had to match my contributions. Suddenly things seemed clearer, but I didn't have a clue as to what was in store for me.

The following month an ad appeared in our diocesan magazine for secretaries for the Episcopal Church Center. I called to inquire about openings and received the usual, "Send us your resume, and we will be in touch." Not very hopeful, I mailed it off the following day.

To my surprise, the personnel officer called me a few days later to arrange an interview. I couldn't believe the feeling I had as I entered the glass doors at 815 Second Avenue. It was as if someone was whispering in my ear, "You're home." After a brief meeting with the personnel officer, and a somewhat longer interview with the Reverend Henry J. Free, Jr., stewardship officer, they offered me a position as his secretary. They felt I was overqualified for that particular position but said they really wanted me on their staff. My concern was that the salary was so much lower than I had been earning at the sign company.

I was alone coming down in the elevator from the third floor personnel office to the lobby. "What shall I do?" I thought. I remembered the tight budget, the doctors' and therapist's bills. Father Free's description of the work I would be doing sounded wonderful.

He and the other people I had met were so gracious. They had shown me a brand new desk and typewriter that would be mine and had introduced me to the other people with whom I would be working. The elevator ride seemed to be taking a very long time. It seemed that time was slowing down or being suspended.

The elevator stopped. No one got on, but it stopped. It wasn't between floors, and no one had signaled from another floor, but the elevator was not moving. The doors did not open, there was no sound, but for some unknown reason I was not afraid. I felt safe. The lights seemed to get much brighter, and I felt warm. Not uncomfortably warm, just cozy and somewhat protected. Suddenly my concerns about money were gone. Surprisingly, my worries about how our family would manage with less income disappeared. My only thought was, "I'll discuss it with Tom." Abruptly the doors opened, and I walked out into the lobby.

While I was preparing dinner that night, I discussed the day with my husband. He couldn't stop smiling. When I asked why, he just said, "Take it!" I didn't even turn from the stove. I kept stirring and giving all the reasons why we couldn't afford for me to take such a big salary cut. He said, "Take it! We will live on whatever we make. This is something I know you should do. Please, Hon, take it. Call them tomorrow."

The warmth that I had felt in the elevator swept over me again. A feeling of being secure and confident surrounded Tom and me in our kitchen as we had dinner. The next morning I did call, and three days later I was sitting at my new desk.

Four months later to the day, Tom was dead. Leukemia. He took ill on May 31 and died on July 9. During that impossibly difficult time, I was enfolded in the heart of a loving, caring Christian community. Long lunch-hour visits to the hospital were never questioned. Lateness was always excused. Pastoral care was everywhere. On the day that Tom died, Father Free and a lunchtime friend were with me at the hospital. Many people from the Center attended the funeral and sent beautiful flowers both to the funeral chapel and to me at home. And more importantly, all through that time, the Sustainer sustained.

I have never regretted the decision that the Holy Spirit, Tom, and I made that day. After four years as secretary in the stewardship office, I was promoted to an appointed position on the Presiding Bishop's staff. I have traveled in the United States and in South and Central America. I have studied with prominent lay and clergy leaders in order to learn and teach about stewardship and mission. My ministry in the stewardship office also encouraged my tithing journey. Tithing has helped me to reaffirm that all I have in this life comes from God and that God will continue to accompany me on my journey.

• • •

I know my grandson will question me again some day soon. My two granddaughters, also unchurched, have inquired about my beliefs and my church affiliations. They too will probe as the years go by. They will probably ask why I worked for the church. Why do I attend church? Why do I believe in God? I hope I can respond more clearly than I have in the past. Or perhaps I will just say again, "I believe. I believe in God, my Creator, Redeemer, Sustainer."

Laura E. Wright

Chapter 11
IN THE MIDDLE

Mary E. (Polly) Wheat

Mary E. (Polly) Wheat, M.D., is director of student health services at Barnard College, Columbia University, New York City. Before entering medical school, she worked for the Bureau of Child Welfare in New York City and as an elementary school teacher with emotionally-disturbed children. Her undergraduate degree is in music. In recent years she has been teaching academic medicine as well as researching women's health issues, publishing her results in journals such as *The American Journal of Preventive Medicine, Journal of the American Geriatric Society*, and the *Annals of Internal Medicine.* Polly's current spiritual practice involves centering prayer and mindfulness meditation, which she also uses with Barnard students. Raised an Episcopalian, she is married to a Methodist minister. Their children, David and Rebecca, ages six and four, keep her *in medias res.*

In the Middle of My Selves

My journey begins here, in the middle, where I am. In my case, the middle of New York City. In our neighborhood the commonality is diversity. Walking down the street I hear Greek, Spanish, Tamil, Arabic, Korean, as well as English. So many ways of speaking, so many ways of bringing order to the moments of our days. How do we understand those who are different? How do we journey together?

A speaker at a conference I recently attended stated that a normal, average person can describe at least a thousand different interacting influences or identities that determine how she perceives the others in her world — gender, ethnicity, age, profession, church, friends, families, clubs, teachers, hobbies. So I, normal and average, must also have these thousand different selves, an inner mirroring of the diversity I see all around me. As I look for the signs that mark my path, each of these selves reveals a different glimpse of my destination, of that which I seek, yet cannot seem to name.

How do I achieve wholeness, integration, and reconciliation of my thousand different selves? My journey moves inward, deep into myself, into soul, the glue that binds body and mind together. Like a plant I put down roots. Only then can blossoms flower. And if I am a potato, or a carrot, the most nourishing part of me is also deep, not even visible on the surface. I must follow Mary's example and ponder, deep in my heart. I must learn to recognize the strangers within, to greet and welcome selves I do not love, to feed and water each part of myself. Yet my interior hospitality is often shallow; I am shy and frightened of so many of my selves. I learn that nourishing each part of myself is hard work, counterintuitive to my comforting image of nurture.

I am a Protestant, a child of the Reformation, and much of my life I have approached this task as a reformer. I need to eliminate doubt, not be angry, not be fearful or insecure. By the time I prune, or weed out each of those things, there isn't much of my garden left. And when I get angry at my spiritual failure, as I inevitably do, then the weed of guilt flourishes. Guilt is the antithesis of wholeness; my selves further fragment.

Finding wholeness means recognizing the parts of myself that demand attention. It means starting from where I am, in the middle (or muddle), accepting that, and then learning how to grow. Jesus' life is my way. There I find all things. Not just the good things but the terrors as well — failure, abandonment, anger, pain, ridicule, death. Nothing, no thing, however horrible, fractured his wholeness or separated him from God. It seems only I can close God out. God will never exclude me from the wholeness of creation. In my garden metaphor, I can refuse to dig beneath the surface, to water, or to fertilize. But God does the growing, not I, and I have no choice about being a seed. Seeds *will* grow, as Henry David Thoreau reminds us. "Though I do not believe that a plant will spring up where no seed has been, I have great faith in a seed. Convince me that you have a seed there, and I am prepared to expect wonders."[1] Jesus' story convinces me that we are all seeds.

In the Middle of My Family

When I married, I sensed very clearly that my spiritual journey, as well as my more mundane happiness, required me to live in relationship. The struggles of love and intimacy with another human being mirror my struggles of love and intimacy with God. In the reflection of another I have learned to see more of my selves. Relationship illuminates the shadows of my isolation, and I see interior walls sequestering selves long buried. I learn that I must delve yet more deeply.

I am now the mother of two small children, and again my world is remade. I am now in the middle of my family. This part of the journey is rooted in dailiness, in a child's ritual, in the miracle of new relationship. There is no choice about digging deeper. One only gets through the day by living moment by moment, and God must be found deep in moments or not at all. Another gift.

I was not prepared for the vulnerability that would come with motherhood. My most powerful symbol of loss and sadness came in a dream during a bad time. It was a dream of my infant son falling from my arms to his death on a cement floor. The love I felt for my son had revealed a wall of fear deep within myself. Allowing myself to face my fear, to feel a nameless, long-sequestered grief, eroded my interior prison freeing a lost, vulnerable self. For my son I was willing to bear the pain that I had not been able to bear for myself. Another step toward wholeness.

My children also teach me about the timelessness of each moment. There is no future; thirty minutes is as long as a year. Now is forever. So I learn to stay present, to experience the small miracles.

Having children lends an urgency to my spiritual journey. If I do not know God, then whom will my children learn to recognize? Whoever I am is one of the first ways they will know God, wherever they may later journey. And whoever my husband and I are together is the relationship that will inform their first images of the family of God. Among my frustrations at the unending demands and energy of small children, I am grateful for the centering that moment-to-moment routines bring. I am grateful to learn how much I can give. I am grateful for the painful vulnerability that fertilizes wholeness. I am grateful for the blessing of watching two very small seeds sprout. I am grateful for the glimpses of God I see through their eyes.

In the Middle of the Church

My journey lies in the middle of the church. On one level this is because it must: I am married to a Methodist minister. To find my spiritual path outside the church would bring complications, conflict, might even risk my marriage. And at the very least it would risk the relationship from which our marriage grows. During dry times the "mustness" has been a burden, church participation another "should" in a life that at those times feels filled with "shoulds." Behind every "should" lies guilt, which one, of course, "shouldn't" feel, and, like the little girl with Morton's salt, I look dizzily inward at the repeating picture of guilt carrying should, carrying guilt, carrying should, ever deeper on a spiritual spiral of despair.

When I look in my dictionary, I see that "should" comes from *sollen*, "to be indebted." Here, for me, is an opening. Indebtedness implies gift, something I have received. If my life is filled with "shoulds," then perhaps it is also filled with gifts. Deep within myself, at the center of the spiral, the external obligation of should spins to show its other side, the acceptance of gift, and gratitude for the particulars of my life.

Now the "mustness" becomes a saving structure, a discipline that encourages me to look within my own life and to keep to my own path. A structure can either restrict me or, conversely, protect me from the predators without. I am saved from the predator of "proving" God exists, which I cannot, and freed for the business of believing. The "mustness" of my marriage forces me to focus on God. The Buddhists say, "There are many paths, but there is only one mountain." Being a minister's wife has encouraged me to focus on the mountain, to recognize those glimpses of truth wherever they appear, yet not to allow them to distract me from my path. From my own awareness of how easily I would have been distracted, of how important the "best" path would be, I have learned tolerance for the paths of others. God can and must speak in many voices to penetrate our human Babel. My job is to recognize my own reality so profoundly that I can see its clear reflection in the lives of others and reveal it in my own.

In the Middle of Community

I had returned to the church before I married a minister. Raised an Episcopalian, in college I had drifted away. No anger, no gnashing of teeth, no crisis of faith; I just stopped listening. Now and then I returned for a Christmas Eucharist, still nourished by the music, the liturgy, the sense of home. After many years a call came. Ed, a close friend from my childhood, from my first church family, was dying of cancer thousands of miles away. I picked out a church from the Yellow Pages and went one Sunday. I thought that was a way of being with Ed on his journey. Very quickly I found that being in relationship with Ed had reopened me to relationship with God, that I was on my own journey.

In this church I found myself in the middle of a community, a place where people were struggling to make visible the kingdom of God where they were, an inner-city neighborhood in San Francisco. The church and the tutoring center shared the sanctuary. Homeless folk were fed and clothed. The church and garden were open as a small oasis for all in the neighborhood. People who had not felt welcomed in other churches, many of us gay or lesbian, made this community their spiritual home. Witnessing this struggle to minister and love in ongoing, daily, practical ways made God and Jesus real to me. I needed to see God in others to know that reality.

I, like many others, found my way there at a time when I had been wounded, and I discovered healing. I was welcomed, loved, comforted, and challenged. From the love of others, I began to trust and love myself again.

When I began to see God in others, I dared to believe that God lived in me as well. Now I understood that the comfort and familiarity I had always experienced in the church service came not from nostalgia but because the God within me heard a call, recognized my need to nurture my soul and spirit, to be reconciled with myself. With this acknowledgment of my God within came a challenge as well. I, too, must be God in the world. I am one of those through whom God must work. "Be perfect, therefore, as your heavenly Father is perfect" (Matt. 5:48). How could I possibly follow such a command?

As I pondered these words of Jesus and learned from prayer and meditation with those in my faith community, I realized that it was Jesus' total integration, his total embrace of every part of himself that revealed his unity with God. No deception, no falsehood, no distraction from God's path, separated him from his center, his God within. This is both my challenge and its answer. My task is to be true, to embrace all parts of myself. Not to hide my self-doubt, my anger, or my fear but to greet each as my teacher. "Nothing is covered up that will not be uncovered, and nothing secret that will not become known. What I say to you in the dark, tell in the light" (Matt. 10:26-27). I am to "be perfect" by accepting and embracing my imperfections, for that is the truth of who I am.

The gift of my own salvation binds me to the church community. Perhaps I, or we, will be signposts for another wanderer, whether or not she knows she is lost.

I do know that women must remain within the church or the church ceases to be the community of God.

In the Middle of the World

Just as we must embrace our own brokenness, we must see the brokenness of the world around us. One in every four marriages involves assault. A third of women in the United States have experienced physical or sexual abuse as children. Twenty-five percent of the children in this, the most wealthy country in the world, live below the poverty line.[2] We struggle with racism, with fear and hatred of what is different. We forget that God's image includes us all, that our task is reconciliation, that we all belong wholly (holy) to God.

Here the inner and the outer journeys intersect. If I am to make visible the kingdom of God on earth, then I must experience the kingdom of God within. How can I trust and embrace the stranger on my street when I cannot even recognize the stranger within myself? So this, too, is the task of our faith community: to pray ourselves and each other into wholeness. When I truly welcome the God within, when I accept God's grace, I am at peace. I know that I am home, that indeed I have never left paradise. Then I can reach out my hand to all my sisters and brothers, for I know that we journey together.

Polly Wheat

Chapter 12

GARDENING FOR SURVIVAL

Ellen Kirby

Ellen Kirby, M.R.E., is the director of Brooklyn GreenBridge, the community outreach program of the Brooklyn Botanic Garden in New York City. She spends much of her time advocating for community horticulture. Previously she was the Botanic Garden's project coordinator for urban composting. For twenty-four years, Kirby was assistant general secretary for the Women's Division, General Board of Global Ministries of The United Methodist Church. In her last position there, she administered the unit that coordinates all social justice programs of the Women's Division. Among her publications are *Women: Over Half the Earth's People* (a study guide) and *Women's Concerns in the Women's Division: Evolution of a Focus (1970-1980)*. She received a Cine Golden Eagle Award for production of the film *Women, Amen!*

*L*ike so many big city dwellers, I grew up in a small city with rural outskirts. My earliest childhood memories include a significant block of time shuttling between our home in town and my grandparents' farmhouse "in the country" ten miles from Winston-Salem, North Carolina, so that my mother could care for her ailing parents.

During these preschool years in the country, I remember deeply disliking two things: weeding between rows of vegetables in the hot summer sun and being alone. I yearned for the company of other children. I looked forward to the time when I could go to school and study. The small, rural Elm Grove Methodist Church was just about the only place I could meet other children.

Little did I realize that the scenery of the beautiful North Carolina piedmont — its rolling green hills and red clay farmland rich with productive nutrients — was deeply implanted in my soul.

Living in New York City for the past twenty-five years has been the biggest contrast one could imagine to those early childhood years close to the soil of rural North Carolina. During the first years in New York, I was attracted to the stimulation of ideas and the tremendous diversity of people and cultures. I was also trying to learn how to combine the demands of being an urban person, a professional worker, a wife, a mother, and an active community member. Balancing these roles and surviving was challenge enough to consume my total energy. Gradually I began to realize that something significant was missing. I started on a journey that has led me "back to the farm" but in the midst of the urban dynamic of people, concrete, issues, and the call to community.

After spending more than twenty-five years first as a seminary student and then professional church worker for The United Methodist Church, I began to feel the emergence of a new vocational calling, a calling that goes back to my roots in the North Carolina farmland but one that is essentially rooted in my spirituality and in the most elemental aspects of my identity as a human being.

It all began with houseplants. I couldn't get enough of them. There weren't enough window sills in our Brooklyn apartment. Gradually there were window boxes, then pots on the fire escapes, then terrariums and special indoor light set-ups. The biggest opportunity arose when the volunteer coordinator at our local church's garden resigned. Without hesitation, I stepped forward to take responsibility for our church garden — the equivalent of four city lots. I had come full circle. The church offered me a place to meet my needs to create, to be outdoors, to do physical work. At the same time in that garden I could serve by nurturing a place for the church and community to meet, to enjoy, and to learn.

For the past ten years, this garden has meant survival for me. It brought balance to my life. I am thankful to the people of the Park Slope United Methodist Church for the opportunity to work in this space. During the winter months I would dream about what could be planted, how it could be designed. I would yearn for the beginnings of spring when I could get my hands in the soil. Since my job with a national church agency required tremendous amounts of travel, I had to plan carefully to find time to get to the garden. Many times in the summer months I would work from 5 to 6:30 on weekday mornings before I went to the office or to the airport. I shall never forget my deep disappointment one Saturday when I arrived to do some major weeding and learned that another group would be holding an event in the garden that would preclude my working. Tears streamed down my face to my great embarrassment.

I thought I was weeping because I could not weed that morning. But in reality my tears reflected the vital place the church garden held for me. Being there meant a great deal more than just weeding. Being there gave me time to reflect on the tough issues of the week before. Being there gave me a sense that something was changing, that something very specific occurred as a result of my labor. Unlike the slow, tedious process of social change in the overwhelming "global garden," working in my church garden gave me an opportunity to bring order out of chaos, even if only to a few square yards.

The garden became my place of meditation, for here I could be alone and reflect on various situations and concerns ranging from the Gulf War to my husband's serious illness to my father's death. I could have my own quiet conversations with God about what mattered most. I experienced the garden as a place of spiritual and physical renewal, a cleansing space where muscles stretched and energy flowed in a true experience of re-creation. I felt an almost mystical experience in the very action of putting my hands into the soil, the very basic element from which and to which all living matter flows.

It was also the place to work side-by-side with others and to hear their stories. It became a place to meet people from the community who used the garden and shared what it meant to them to walk by this place of beauty and replenish their spirits. It also became a place of healing for others who worked there during their own stressful times. One man volunteered when he became unemployed and needed some physical work to get his mind off his problems. Some of his deep pain was relieved by coming several times a week to clear up several huge and thorny overgrown shrubs.

Gradually, the garden offered possibilities for environmental education for our local church. The activities of the garden began to coincide with the sermons of our ecologically oriented pastor, the Reverend A. Finley Schaef. When I first began to coordinate the garden, I realized that the condition of the soil was terrible. Since our church was very small, we could not afford to have truckloads of new topsoil delivered, so I learned about composting from one of our church members who had been a Peace Corps volunteer in Latin America. Soon I learned that I didn't have to bag up all the weeds we produced; rather I could put them in our new compost pile and, bingo, in three months we would have rich humus — especially if I mixed the weeds with the accumulated fall leaves.

Then I got the idea that church people could bring their kitchen vegetable and fruit scraps to add to the compost, and we would have even more fresh rich soil to add to the quality of our earth. We now have three compost bins and completely revitalized soil. In the past ten years, we have recycled more than twenty tons of organic materials.

In 1991 the New York City Sanitation Department chose our neighborhood as the city's first Intensive Recycling Zone. They began to pick up compostable kitchen waste at curbside as part of the plan to reduce New York's waste by fifty percent by the year 2000. A significant twenty-block segment of Park Slope, Brooklyn, became the first urban community in the United States to do this. I believe that our church's composting helped set the stage for this major citywide composting effort.

In July 1993, I began a new career at the Brooklyn Botanic Garden as coordinator of urban composting for the borough of Brooklyn with its nearly three million residents. Working with community gardens, schools, religious institutions, housing projects, cemeteries, parks, and private homeowners, I encourage people and institutions to practice composting with the goal of reducing solid waste. In 1994 my work expanded when I became director of Brooklyn GreenBridge, a new program in community outreach of the Brooklyn Botanic Garden.

I have come from tending my houseplants to community composting and gardening. I have also come through a dramatic career change from one challenging job to another. For me, this journey has included an active prayer life, the continuous practice of journaling, taking seriously my inner voice, reaching out to others for counsel, and developing a strong sense of my value as a human being. Many times as I have cried out to God for an answer to the question, "What shall I do?" The answer has always come in opportunities for involvement, in friends who appeared with support, in insights gained from study and reflection. Never would I have imagined ten years ago when I first learned about composting that I would be working to find ways to involve the whole borough of Brooklyn.

Because of this experience, I dream about the church as a place where people from all walks of life find interesting and challenging ways to serve their community, where women's and men's talents are equally shared and recognized, where faith and action are integrated into tangible expressions of social healing. I dream about the church as a living witness to society of the most important messages of love and justice that the Christ presence in and among us can offer. I dream of a church that witnesses with concrete actions to the right relationship between human beings and the soil, air, and water that sustain the whole planet.

The church gardening provided a location for me to experiment, to learn, and to create. It enabled me to discover a new vocation while remaining grounded in the same call to mission in God's world. Through this experience of personal transformation, I learned to trust the deepest questions that flowed from my call to new directions. I learned to live patiently with the questions.

I continue to hope that the church will provide the same nurturing climate for a multitude of others to follow their dreams. I hope my story will provide encouragement for the search.

SECTION FOUR

PASTORS

"Mary Magdalene went and
announced to the disciples,
'I have seen the Lord.' "

John 20:18a

Chapter 13

HAVE SOME MORE, DARLINGS! THERE'S PLENTY!

Margaret Guenther

Margaret Guenther, Ph.D., is director of the Center for Christian Spirituality, and professor of ascetical theology at The General Seminary, New York City. Her first career was teaching Germanic languages and literatures at the university level. Since her ordination to the priesthood in the Episcopal church in 1984, she has been a frequent lecturer, preacher, conductor of retreats and quiet days. When not engaged in seminary teaching and the ministry of spiritual direction, Margaret herself retreats to an old farmhouse in the Virginia Blue Ridge to write books such as *Holy Listening: The Art of Spiritual Direction* (1992). She has in the works now with Cowley Publications a still-untitled book on the spirituality of the second half of life.

*T*he suggestion that I reflect on my life in the church was like an invitation to embark on an exploratory trip into the tangled jungles of unawareness of the past, the broad savannahs of bland and blind observance, the occasional cliffs and swamps of crisis and despair. What I found also was a table set for dinner and surrounded by gathered kin.

I was baptized in 1929. Since I was an infant, I have no memory of the event, but I am assured that I was a winsome, well-behaved baby. In other words, I did not put up a fuss.

Since that Sunday morning in a Midwestern Presbyterian congregation, the church has been central to my life. With greater or lesser degrees of enthusiasm, I have been faithful. In my decades of lay ministry, I participated in all manner of good works and sat on myriad committees. In my fiftieth year, something quite unexpected happened: I abandoned my previously comfortable and satisfying life as a college teacher and began the process toward ordination in the Episcopal church. To a casual observer it might have looked as if I were experiencing a midlife crisis — which, in a way, I was — but more importantly, I was just beginning to *live* my faith, to explore it, to test its boundaries.

The path toward ordination was not easy. Our culture's suspicions regarding "older women," while unacknowledged and often unconscious, run deep. I did not look like a priest — I looked like someone's mother. Why, I was asked, couldn't I just go on doing what I had been doing?

I don't know why, but I couldn't. I knew that I was called to the priesthood, and I knew that a denial of that call would be a denial of life itself. Of course, I would go on living, go on putting one foot in front of the other, but a vital spark would have been extinguished before it had a chance to burst into flame.

Somehow I survived the selection process, convincing the skeptical screeners of the validity of my call and of my possible usefulness to the church. I was disappointed that my decades of faithful observance seemed to count for nothing and that the absence of traumatic incidents was viewed with suspicion that I had never really lived. But somehow I survived, was ordained, and am now a member of a seminary faculty.

The Web of Connection

Very early in my priesthood I had a Eucharistic vision — possibly in unconscious imitation of my spiritual sisters of the High Middle Ages, who were given to vivid and sometimes alarming imaginings during the celebration of the Sacrament. It took me by surprise: I am committed to the celebration of the liturgy "by the book," in other words, as carefully and lovingly as possible but with no place for the unexpected or the unexplained —   except, of course, for that inexplicable mystery which *is* the sacrament.

But this time I suddenly found myself tempted to ad lib during the institution narrative. As I prepared to say the words, "Take, eat," I heard a maternal voice from somewhere deep in my subconscious. It was not a youthful voice, nor did it sound like the voice of a thin woman. The voice — warm, inviting, and infinitely giving — said: "Have some more, darlings! There's plenty! Have seconds!" For just a moment I wanted to repeat her words in her tone as I elevated the paten and then the chalice. I wanted the Eucharist to be a great family feast — much too much ever to be consumed, the table laden with everybody's favorite foods and with no thought at all of calories or cholesterol.

I didn't succumb to the temptation. I remained proper and by the book, but I knew that I had been graced with a glimpse of what it's all about, *really*. And I knew that my priesthood needed to reflect that vision of overwhelming abundance and prodigal generosity.

And I thought: Maybe this is what women can bring to the priesthood. Maybe we can bring the housewifely and the maternal, the web of connection rather than the ladder of ascent, the affective rather than the logical.

Where Were the Role Models?

I grew up in a corner of the church where God most clearly resembled his picture on the ceiling of the Sistine Chapel —   patriarchal, stern, and just but certainly not very cuddly. Jesus was there too, his relationship not very clear despite the weekly recitation of the Apostles' Creed. He was friendlier than God, certainly more approachable, but definitely second-string. He had the reputation of liking children. I remember a large picture in the third-grade Sunday school classroom, where he sat on a big rock and embraced well-washed and attractive children of assorted skin colors. He seemed to mean well, but I thought: Why doesn't he get down on the ground and *play* with them if he likes them as much as he says? Maybe those impractical garments inhibit free movement.

Women were nowhere to be seen. That is to say, they were nowhere to be seen as liturgical or congregational leaders. They were highly visible in the pews, the parish kitchen, and the Sunday school. They sang in the choir, but they did not proclaim the Word.

Nor were they present among the cloud of witnesses. The church of my childhood was nervous of saints, so I grew up without the supportive sisterhood of women who had gone before me. Lustily I sang "Faith of Our Fathers" and knew nothing of Perpetua and Felicity, Teresa of Avila (now *there* was a strong woman!), or Julian of Norwich — to say nothing of my dragon-slaying name-sake Margaret of Antioch, and Martha of Bethany, who did not slay the dragon but rather subdued it and used it in her service. Silently, almost unconsciously, I envied my Roman Catholic friends who had gracious and beautiful Mary to keep them company in church. In my own circles she was regarded with great suspicion and permitted to make brief appearances only on Christmas cards. Even then, too great a preoccupation with nativity scenes was regarded as "Catholic" and hence theologically suspect.

So it was a masculine, patriarchal faith. It's hard now to believe that no one seemed to question it. It's hard now to contemplate all the questions that never got asked, that were maybe pushed down into the subconscious at their first stirrings. How did Sarah feel when Abraham got the orders to leave the security of home and move out into the unknown, to say nothing of how she felt when he took Isaac on that walk up Mt. Moriah? Did her husband tell her what he was up to, or was it a private deal between him and God? Did Mary feel appropriately grateful to Joseph when he, being a just man and unwilling to expose her to shame, resolved to divorce her quietly, then changed his mind when he got a direct command from an angel? Or did she feel used and patronized? And the regal unnamed woman who anointed Jesus' head in Mark's Gospel — how did she get conflated with the penitent sinner groveling on the floor in Luke's account, washing his feet with her tears and drying them with her hair? Why did little girls of my generation grow up knowing all about the woman on the floor and nothing about her prophet-sister?

Who cooked the Last Supper? And what about the women at the tomb, especially in Mark's account, those women who said nothing to anyone because they were afraid? How can the Gospel writer's curt dismissal fit with their courage as watchers at the foot of the cross? Surely, anyone who has watched a crucifixion would not be so easily frightened, certainly not at the opportunity to be the bearer of good news. And who were all those women mentioned in Paul's letters? Despite his reputation for misogyny, he clearly valued their competence and faithfulness. Yet all those teaching me about the early church portrayed it as a band of brothers.

To put all this in the jargon of our time, *where were my role models?*

I remember being asked that question when, in my fiftieth year, I sought admission to seminary and the ordination process. The question took me aback — I thought briefly of Mother Teresa, not because I foresaw a ministry like hers but because she was the only woman older than I whom I could think of at the moment. But she was not the answer, so I struggled for a reply and felt shame at my incoherence.

I suspect the question was asked as a standard interviewing ploy, something to get the conversation started or to keep it going. Yet that question — Who are your role models? — was far more pivotal than my interviewer could have imagined. And my own incoherence, my own lack of clarity was far more than a sign of social embarrassment. The question challenged my then-unexamined images of God and church. Taken seriously, it forced me to look at the great family album of the saints living and dead and then to ask myself: Where is your kinship? Who and what do you want to be when you grow up?

I realize now that I could not answer because I honestly did not *know*. In 1979 when I entered seminary, the ordination of women to the priesthood in the Episcopal church was still very new, but the struggle preceding the final vote had gone on for so long that I did not feel like a pioneer. I assumed that a woman would undergo a process of formation and study and then be ordained — just like a man. It would be, I thought, not so very different from my attendance at graduate school twenty-five years previously when women were a tolerated minority working hard to fit into an essentially patriarchal system. A priest is a priest is a priest, after all.

"What Shall We Call You?"

A priest *is* a priest, but in the years since my interviewer inadvertently directed me to look deep into myself and into the institution representing God on earth, I have become aware of the complexity, ambiguity, and richness of my relationship with the church.

It is complex and ambiguous because, as a priest, I am the same as my brothers, yet different. Vestments and traditional clerical dress can take away individuality, even gender. Yet no one would mistake me for a man, even when I stand at the altar with identically garbed male colleagues, even when my singing voice is most comfortable in the tenor range, even when my words and gestures come straight from *The Book of Common Prayer* and *The Priest's Handbook*.

Sometimes the reaction to a woman priest is curiosity, sometimes discomfort. This is most obviously manifested in the question: "What shall we call you? Surely not 'Father'! How about 'Reverend'?" I usually suggest that I am comfortable with the use of my Christian name (which is probably what God calls me) without any honorific. But when I am pressed for a title, in circles where my male colleagues are addressed as "Father," I suggest "Mother" as the consistent, truly parallel title. I have yet to meet a parishioner or retreatant who considers this a good idea!

(I am not sure that I like it myself, just as I am uncomfortable with the use of "Father." It seems much healthier for us to be brothers and sisters. Or perhaps we should get away from family imagery altogether and identify ourselves as friends and companions. Companions, after all, are those who share bread.)

For the time being, however, many of us move in circles where male clergy are called "Father." Where does that leave me as a woman? I certainly don't want more children — three biological ones are quite sufficient. But I *am* a mother; I know about mothering in the very marrow of my bones, in my blood, in the deepest places of my soul. I bring the experience of mothering to my priesthood — in my ability to put myself aside and pay attention to another, in my ability to enter into another's pain without being consumed by it, in my ability to go on hoping when a situation seems hopeless. The experience of motherhood has even shaped me in less spiritual ways: Good administration is not too different from good family management, in which members are encouraged to take responsibility for themselves and in which they feel loved and valued.

So as a priest, I am indeed a mother, even though I would prefer to be called something else! And I ponder: Perhaps a model of healthy motherhood isn't so bad! And perhaps this kind of mothering has little to do with biological parenting: One need not have borne children to partake of it.

Is There a Place for Us?

As a priest, I also find myself an apologist for the church to other women. My ministry has evolved into one of teaching and spiritual direction. Increasingly, those who seek me out are women, women who love the church and are drawn to its service but who have been hurt or at least minimized by the institution. Clergy, seminarians, members of religious orders, and laity — they all bring essentially the same question to our conversations: How can I be faithful to God and to my own deepest self in this institution that so often seems to have no place for me?

Seminarians chafe under the masculine language of the prayer book, to say nothing of the patriarchal imagery of the Victorian Gothic stained glass windows in our chapel. There are a few women depicted, to be sure, but most of them are kneeling on the floor, humble and subservient. The more-than-lifesize statues behind the altar show Christ as the Good Shepherd, flanked by an assortment of apostles, Moses, and Elijah. There is a reliable rumor that several years ago a small statue of Mary was hidden behind the central figure of Christ, but I lack the agility and opportunity to climb up behind the high altar to investigate. Knowing that she is there is comforting, however, and I rejoice when the secret of her presence is passed on to each new generation of women students.

My clergy sisters struggle too with language but struggle even more to be taken seriously. To be petite, pretty, and well dressed risks tacit dismissal as "a cute little thing." To be large and unconcerned with fashion risks dismissal of another sort — who wants such an unattractive and unfeminine priest? Too soft-spoken? You lack authority. Too loud? You are strident. Even as I searched for my own role models fifteen years ago, ordained women are still grappling with the issue of public identity. How can they respond to the inner, compelling call to God's service, remain true to themselves, and minister effectively within the institution? What to wear is not an idle question for appearance sends a powerful message. Earrings at the altar? Nail polish? Clerical collar or brightly colored scarf around my neck? And does it *always* have to be a sensible black suit?

Then there are the "ordinary" women, the women in the pews, the women who keep parishes alive. Like their seminarian and clergy sisters, they too are struggling with questions of identity and vocation. They too are concerned with their stewardship of time, energy, and creativity. They too look at the institution with emotions ranging from ambivalence through disappointment and disillusion to deep and undisguised hostility. They too are trying to sort out what God has to do with the church, and vice versa. They too are living with the tension of remaining in the church and loving it while remaining keenly aware of its injustices and shortcomings.

Counseling Subversion

My conversations with all these women, whether or not they are officially labeled "spiritual direction," are at the heart of my ministry. Together we laugh, cry, rage, and sigh. Behind closed doors we practice a little creative heresy — and live to tell of it. Together we explore the territory, test the boundaries, and expand the horizon.

And again and again, I find myself counseling *subversion*. Subversion as a way of being has been maligned and vastly neglected, associated with espionage and assorted nefarious doings. (The good guys, the ones on *our* side, are rarely presented as subversives: They are fighters for goodness and truth.) Yet in its literal meaning, subversion connotes turning *downward, under*. For me this means turning to that deep inner place of fertile darkness, the neglected place of mystery and imagination. For me, subversion can indeed mean turning the world upside down — not in the sense of political disruption but in the sense of new vision, of looking at the seemingly familiar with totally new eyes. Subversion means letting go of preconceptions; it means trusting God's love sufficiently to risk the changes imperative with new insights.

So when I counsel subversion, I do not mean infiltration of diocesan offices (although that might be a good idea!), nor do I mean overthrow of the institution as we know it (although institutions can become the object of idolatry and hence merit our critical attention). Rather, I counsel a fearless and joyful exploration downward into the neglected and the unknown depths of a woman's faith. I urge my sisters to get acquainted (or reacquainted) with the saints. There are some strong, beautiful, eccentric, powerful women in the family album. There are visionaries such as Hildegard of Bingen and skilled administrators such as Hilda of Whitby. Our own century has brought us the rich variety of Therese of Lisieux (well, almost — she died in 1897), Edith Stein, and Dorothy Day. And of course saints don't really have to be on anybody's official list — our own mothers, grandmothers, aunts, and teachers might serve as models.

Further, I urge women to read Scripture with new eyes, through the lens of subversion. Feminist scholars such as Elisabeth Moltmann-Wendel and Virginia Ramey Mollenkott provide help in seeing what has been there all along.[1] We need to reclaim Sophia and the feminine aspect of the Holy Spirit. We need to submerge ourselves in the neglected feminine imagery for God. We would find that nothing is taken away but that great richness is added.

And I urge women to find and trust their voices. All too often, we are given answers to questions we never asked, and we stifle the questions that well up within us. Women in positions of leadership need to speak and write in their own voices: The language of patriarchy is no longer obligatory. Many of us were trained to be bilingual. A second language is always a useful skill but never at the cost of forgetting one's native tongue.

There's Plenty!

There are days when I despair of the church, when the institution seems stale and rigid, when the gospel seems forgotten. But I am heartened — paradoxically enough — by looking back at its history. The track record of the institution is *not* good. One need think only of the Inquisition, the myriad forcible conversions, the centuries of persecution of women as witches, the subjugation of indigenous peoples by "Christian" conquerors, the many instances of complicity with cruel and unjust regimes.

No, the history of Christ's church on earth, while it has its glorious moments, is enough to make the angels weep. But the church goes on; the church is alive.

It is still not an easy place for women, at least not for women who refuse to be afraid and silent, unlike the passive women of Mark's resurrection account. We are still looking for our role models, our sisters to guide us, to beckon us on, to encourage and challenge us. We are provided sustenance when we turn downward and inward, when we commit ourselves to holy subversion. Companions to each other as we explore the depths, we no longer need look afar for our role models: We find them in ourselves.

But the church is alive, and women continue to feel the irresistible tug to commitment. They continue to be drawn, even to face diminishment and discouragement, as they offer themselves to its service. I can explain to myself its survival, its mysterious attractiveness only by an image and a voice. It is the comforting image of a great family feast and the maternal voice that says, "Have some more, darlings! There's plenty! Have seconds!"

Margaret B. Guenther

Chapter 14
WHY WOULD A SELF-RESPECTING FEMINIST BE A CHRISTIAN?

Patricia Wilson-Kastner

Patricia Wilson-Kastner, Ph.D., is the rector of the Church of St. Ann and the Holy Trinity, Brooklyn. She presently serves as the president of the board of the St. Ann's Center for the Arts. She holds several positions in the diocese of Long Island as well as being a member of the national Standing Commission on Ecumenical Relations and the international Anglican-Methodist Dialogue Group. In the recent past she was the Trinity Church Professor of Preaching at The General Theological Seminary in Manhattan. Fortress Press has published three of her books: *Faith, Feminism, and the Christ* (1983); *Imagery for Preaching* (1989); and *Pentecost 3: Proclamation 5, Series B* (1994).

The Question

"Why do I stay in the church?" The question is immediate and personal. It is a radically individual query that affects me every day. My religious beliefs, my spirituality, my occupation, my sense of purpose are all bound up in my response. I am not answering the question, "Why ought one to remain in the church?" or "Why might one continue in the church?" but "Why do I remain?"

At the same time, my statement of belonging is public. To belong to a worldwide organization such as the church binds one with other people all over the globe in a common allegiance. It would be hubris to pretend to be very important to all or even many of those people, but to leave the church or to stay, with all my feelings and reasoning, speaks to other people, to encourage, to discourage, or to disturb. My belonging and my experiences are part of a global tapestry. My decision to stay in or to leave the church will transform, albeit so modestly, the pattern being woven.

Thus, in this context, I respond to the question "Why do I stay in the church?" both for myself and for my brothers and sisters. To begin, I will briefly raise up my experience, shared by so many, of both affirmation and rejection in the church. Then I want to explain, as simply as I can, why I stay in the Episcopal church, as a baptized member who is a priest and rector of a parish.

The Saga

Probably the most important theme of my life in the church is strong attraction and and equally intense experience of rejection. I grew up as a Roman Catholic. When I was a child, four or five, I wanted to be a priest. I preached to the cats and claimed a blanket as my chasuble. Quickly, I was told bluntly that girls could not be priests. There was, however, an alternative. I could be a member of a religious order. I might be a nun.

So I was introduced to the alternating rhythm of my life in the church: You can't do this because we don't do that, but we have something else for you to do which is also important, even if not what you want to do.

I was also fascinated by the church as an institution although I would never have used the word. Our neighborhood was pretty rough, but the parish church and the school were places of relative order and beauty. When I graduated from high school, I joined the religious community that had taught me and spent six years there, from 1962 to 1968. These were the years of the excitement and turmoil of Vatican II. The atmosphere I imbibed in my community suggested that the church could be different, more faithful to its biblical roots and its rich and varied tradition, and that I was responsible for doing my part to change the church.

After having left the convent because of the community's refusal to practice the social theology of the church, as I believed I had been taught it, I began graduate work in theology: an M.A. at the University of Dallas and then a Ph.D. at the School of Religion at the University of Iowa. At Iowa I became acquainted with the United Church of Christ and found it a haven. It encouraged my religious questioning and was vastly more accepting of me as a woman theologian than the Roman Catholic church was. I was ordained in the United Church and taught for several years at its seminary in Minneapolis. There I became much more deeply involved in feminist theology and convinced that the equal participation of women and men in the church was a matter of theological necessity, not just convenience or civil justice.

The UCC was much more accepting of me as a woman, but what I soon found missing in my life in the UCC was the liturgical and theological seriousness I valued. I discovered that I could be as radical a feminist as I wanted, but I wouldn't be taken seriously by most of my colleagues if I wished to discuss the sacramental presence of Christ in the church or the theological and liturgical significance of the metaphor of God as Mother.

About 1975 I became reacquainted with the Episcopal church, with which I had had some contact in Texas. With its vote to ordain women in 1976, I saw an opening to a Christian community more congenial to my beliefs and to the practice of ministry I sought. I have belonged to the Episcopal church since 1979. It would be false to say "and she lived happily ever after." I have experienced blatant sexism in my own treatment as a woman priest, a growing withdrawal of the church from its commitment to radical biblical social teachings, and an increasing preoccupation with semi-theological debates about sexuality at the cost of ignoring other issues from the Incarnation to our very theology of the church.

However, I have stayed in the Episcopal church and cannot imagine leaving it. It is the branch of Christianity in which I believe that I belong. Despite its shortcomings, in this church I am encouraged to live the gospel faithfully. Despite the church's sexism (amid its other faults), I can live in and toward the new creation to which the gospel calls us. How can any self-respecting feminist claim that?

The Prejudices

Before I respond to that question, which I frequently ask myself, I would underscore that this church is not paradise for women. Sexism still lives, in our structures and in the individuals who have internalized it. As professor in a seminary, I have encountered prejudice in colleagues and in students. As a rector I have had people leave the parish because they could not accept a woman as their pastor. When I was a candidate for bishop in a reputedly liberal midwestern diocese, clergy and laity commented that they could not support me because I was too short to be a bishop. "Why vote for a woman," asked others, "when there are three handsome male candidates?"

These superficial responses, masking a deep sexism that hides its identity, form a part of the ongoing experience that forces me to ask if the church is worth the pain, the dehumanizing experiences, and the demeaning attitudes of so many people who identify themselves as Christians. My modest experiences are as nothing compared to those who have experienced the church sanctifying abusive marriages, refusing to hear the cries of those who have been victimized by those acting in the church's name, and denying the need to labor for the full equality of women in society and church. I certainly could not remain in the church if I valued it only as a human community, or could simply say, "Well, I've met worse."

Ultimately, when I am most challenged by the sexism of the church, I go back to the radical questions at the heart of theology. Do I believe that God is? Do I believe that God cares about creation and about humanity? Do I believe that faith is an encounter with a reality that can rightly be called both profoundly, immanently present in this world and also radically transcendent to my desires and my understandings? Do I believe that this God is in any way present and accessible in and through the church?

The Heart of the Matter

For me, the existential core of the matter is that I find a divine presence, both comforting and challenging, at the heart of the church's life. The church may betray, and indeed has most grievously betrayed, that divine Life, as I, on a smaller scale, may myself be unfaithful to my truest self and my ideals. But the divine Presence remains, even amid our human infidelity.

We humans can misuse our freedom in order to enslave and degrade others. Sexism is perhaps the most basic manifestation of that human evil behavior. One of my moments of feminist illumination came when I read Phyllis Trible's *Texts of Terror*,[1] when I saw this radical abuse woven into the story of human creativity as a distortion of the human equality and interconnectedness for which God created humanity.

This mythic insight provides me with a perspective to express both the vision of human cooperation and community that fulfills the best in us, and our abusive resistance to the good that we might realize in our world's life. I have preferred to focus on a global vision of what we might be, while recognizing the brutal reality that can prevent us from being what we might be, what our humanity is intended to be. The evil that oppresses us comes from without and but also grows within us. It is an evil I choose to struggle against.

However, I do not believe that sexism, that paradigmatic expression of our evil mistreatment of each other, is intrinsic to Christianity, religion, or even to men. Thus my reasons for being a Christian and remaining within the church, rest in my faith in God and a goodness in humanity and our freedom. My frustration with the church consequently relates to my conviction that the church is unfaithful to itself and to God in being sexist. I can understand well why some people find the church's infidelity and attachment to its own sexist betrayal of the gospel so appalling that they would choose to reject the church.

The Hope

I am more hopeful. My confidence is based as much or more on the church's possibilities as on its consistent performance. Four specific aspects of the church make it possible for me to stay: The presence of God in the church, what the church can do for humanity, the grandeur and the squalor of our history, and a worldwide community. None of them alone might be enough; all of them keep me here.

I have already written of my sense of the presence of God in the church. Of course God can be found elsewhere in many guises. But God is present, I am convinced, in and through the church. Through the church I learned about God, began to interpret my experiences of God, was taught how others through the ages had experienced God, and as a happy by-product, was offered many positive models of women as respected and active. Even if these ideals are not now entirely satisfactory to me, they gave me a strong and good beginning, and directed me to areas for further growth.

The Christian faith also assumes that faith, personal behavior, and the life of the globe are all interconnected. Christian ethics is rooted in a belief in the goodness of creation accompanied by an acknowledgment of our brokenness and of the human need for transformation. In this context, our redemption is the realization of the fullest human good for all humanity, respecting the life of all creation as a part of humanity's role in creation.

Christianity has evolved a powerful set of symbols and rituals to motivate and encourage people in this behavior. As with the issue of sexism, our problem is not so much that the ideals are flawed but that we have not practiced them. Perhaps more to the point, the church has allowed itself to accept a muting of its ideals for social acceptance. For instance, the church has allowed itself to be the sanctifier of sexist behavior instead of applying the dynamic of the biblical vision of human community in prophetic critique of society. I want to hear this prophetic voice more loudly crying; we have seen in places such as South Africa its struggle to transform the very depths of society as well as personal behavior.

The church is a human community filled with foul deeds, glorious episodes, and much mediocrity. Some people are driven away from the church because of its mixed history. Personally, I find this much more real than dedication to fantasies or disembodied ideals. Real people's lives are messy, and so is the church. Personally I find myself rather reassured with our growing awareness of so much of the good and the evil in our history, and our struggle with our ideals. Women's history has been most helpful in bringing out our hidden history in the church.

Although I suppose one can use the data of history as one chooses, I have always been surprised with how much has gone right, given the possibilities for chaos and abuse. Perhaps that is a temperamental issue. I, for one, find women's history in the church a source of great encouragement at the power of women's spirits in the face of such adversity. (I am always encouraged if we seem to be working on, or even have succeeded in, ridding ourselves of some of the evils that have oppressed women.)

I remain in the church because it is a worldwide community. Through direct personal contact, writing, and prayer, we are connected with each other. We support and critique each other as we all search to be faithful. I am horrified, for example, at the words spoken in discussion at Lambeth by a Ugandan bishop who asserted that women ought not to be ordained because women can be sold as wives. In his view, because they are chattel, they are not worthy to be ordained as priests. However, he reminds me of my own history as part of a people who sold his relatives into slavery and participated in chopping up and rearranging his area of the world in accord with our colonialist convenience. I do not wish to acquiesce in his sexism; I want all of us to be more respectful of each other and to stop standing on each others' necks (to echo the Grimké sisters).

I hope that all of us will live in the communion to which God has called us. I believe that we humans are one people, part of a living world. God gave us humans the ability and responsibility not only to be one community but also to live in the divine life and energy that can bind us in love. This vision is a challenge to us. The church is the place where I can be challenged and comforted as a part of that global community, in which we together can struggle with God's call to us. Even if I am not always happy with developments, even if I am sometimes mistreated by this church, it is also a powerful source of life for me, and I intend to stay.

Patricia Wilson-Kastner

Chapter 15

FROM CRISIS TO CREATIVE ENERGY

Susan Cole

Susan Cole, M.Div., is co-pastor of Arch Street United Methodist Church, a multiracial congregation in downtown Philadelphia. Her previous pastorates have included Calvary United Methodist Church and Emmanuel United Methodist Church, both also in Philadelphia. Currently she serves her denomination as vice-chair of the Board of Ordained Ministry of the Eastern Pennsylvania Annual Conference. Susan has written, with Marian Ronan and Hal Taussig, *Sophia: The Future of Feminist Spirituality* (1986) and *Wisdom's Feast: Sophia in Study and Celebration* (1989), both published by Harper & Row. She leads workshops on "Sophia, the Wisdom of God" and "Wisdom's Ways: Spiritual Exercises for Women."

I am a United Methodist clergywoman and a feminist. I was brought up in the church, and I love it. It nurtured me from childhood; it's where I have been called to serve in ministry. But I am torn in my feelings for the church; I am disturbed at how hard it has been to grow spiritually within its narrow confines and how harsh it has been to me and others who see things differently.

When I think about how I have related to the church in the past decade, it is clear to me that what holds me within the church and the hope that I hold out for the church's future is my relationship to Sophia. Sophia is the Wisdom of God, the divine imaged as female, who is found within the Bible and within Christian tradition.[1] She has become my primary divine image; she is a source of strength, wonder, and joy. Through her I have discovered in whole new ways divine presence within myself, within my sisters, within all that is. She has made a profound difference in my life and is beginning to make a difference in the church.

As brief introduction, Sophia is a transliteration of the Greek word for "wisdom." In English translations of the biblical text she is called Wisdom. I prefer Sophia because it is a woman's name, and she is clearly depicted as female. It is her female imagery that is most distinctive and creative for me.

Spiritual Crisis

I first experienced Sophia's power in my life at a time when I was in crisis regarding my ministry. The United Methodist Church ordains women and is among the most progressive denominations in welcoming women into leadership. Even so, being a clergywoman is not easy. Although there has been slow, steady progress on such issues as gaining recognition, authority, status, and pay on an equal basis with men, women still have a ways to go. My personal crisis came in an even more difficult area: spirituality. Spirituality in the church has been formed from a predominantly male point of view. Images of God, ways of worshiping, religious experiences have left out the female point of view for centuries.

My struggle was how to be a leader in a church where my own spirituality didn't quite fit, where I found myself struggling with the possibility of losing my soul to fit into a male system. At that time, it felt as though I were on my way out of the church simply because there was not enough room for my understanding and experience of faith. I was working hard to undo the male God language and imagery, and to find new language and imagery to hold my evolving faith, all the while ministering to folk in a position that carries with it the expectation that I had my own spiritual house somewhat in order. Working too hard, with not enough room to breathe freely, I was in danger of spiritual asphyxiation. Like many clergy sisters before and since, I began to question my calling and my faith.

I remember one particular time when I was together with good women friends doing a reflection on the Bible passage about the ten wise and foolish virgins (Matt. 25:1-15). In my meditation on the passage, I put myself into the story. There I was, rushing to fill my lamp with oil after it ran dry, running back to be in time to meet Jesus, and my lamp turned into a sieve, the oil running out as fast as I was running to be on time. Sharing that meditation sent me into a painful examination of my life in ministry. How could I be a minister proclaiming Jesus Christ when I couldn't keep my own lamp filled? My energy, my spirit, my life was draining out through the holes in the sieve. What was the point of serving the church if it was killing me?

Another image that occurred regularly during that time was of me perched on the very edge of the church, on a precipice. I vacillated between the danger of being pushed over the edge out into the void that lay beyond, and the danger of spiritual death if I didn't go ahead and jump over the edge myself.

Finally, things came apart right in the middle of a worship service — while I was celebrating Communion, the most important act of my ministry. In the middle of the service I began to stumble over the words. I found myself asking how I could be celebrating the life of a man — how I could be lifting up someone whom I could never be like. All of what I knew about our oneness as the body of Christ left me. There I was, passing out the elements, stuttering over the words, with questions swirling around in my head. It was devastating. I was certain that I had no option but to leave the church.

It was in the midst of this spiritual crisis that Sophia came to me. The following week on the eve of Epiphany, more than ten years ago now, sitting in my own living room in front of the fire, I was preparing a worship service. While I was writing a prayer, Sophia appeared in a vision. She appeared as a dark-haired, dark-eyed woman, laughing. With mocking laughter, as if to discount all of my agonizing, she began to tell me that she had been with me since before I was born, that I was very precious to her. She said there was no way I was unfaithful since she had always known me and been with me. Then she called me to follow her, saying we had a lot to do, and was gone.

Tears came immediately, tears of joy and relief. Sophia came laughing at my crisis of faith and left me crying at the experience of this new-found presence in my life. That moment marked a profound shift in my sense of who God was and where God was. Until then, God had been male, located out beyond me somewhere. I wanted a different image of God and had tried hard to rid myself of that image — only to be left with dryness, a spiritual void. With Sophia, God came as female, someone like me, someone that affirmed every bit of who I was, someone that knew me through and through. After the vision was over, she didn't leave. I felt her presence in my body. She not only was like me, she dwelled within me. I had always loved 1 John 4:16b — "God is love, and those who abide in love abide in God, and God abides in them" — but I never really felt it. After Sophia's appearance, I felt it within me. When I thought about responding to her call to follow her, it felt as though I was both following her while still being very connected. It was, and continues to be, a physical sensation, as though I were tied to her, almost like an umbilical cord connecting us. Even now, more than a decade later, the thought of that moment fills me with gratitude.

Sophia's Answer

Sophia's appearance didn't solve the question of whether to leave the church or not. I thought that perhaps following her would mean leaving the church, but I wasn't certain. A week or two later, in a meditation, I sought an answer to that question. I saw myself in a large, narrow Gothic church. At the front, off to the side, a door was open, and Sophia called to me through that open door. I felt my heart sink as I followed, thinking, *Well, here's my answer — it's out of the church for me.* I went out into a vast, bright summer meadow ringed with trees. There were all kinds of people around, some dancing, some flying kites, enjoying themselves, children playing. A vast, lacy dome spanned the sky, right to the horizon. This was Sophia's church! Expansive, bright, airy, including the natural world and a variety of people and activities. I looked back at the church from which I'd come and discovered that the church was right there, under the dome, a part of Sophia's church. That's when I got my answer. Yes, I could stay in ministry within the church because it was a part of Sophia's larger world; and yes, I could leave ministry because I would still be following Sophia. The choice was mine; Sophia offered me the wideness of creation to follow her in whatever way was best for me.

I have chosen to stay in the church. My roots are there; it has been the primary source of my nourishment, my values, and my stance in life. Narrow and flawed though it is, the church is where I come from. What Sophia has done for me in my stance within the church is to give me both the personal strength to bring all of myself to an institution that is threatened by women being themselves and a whole new way of looking at my tradition with Sophia as part of the mix.

Creative Energy

After experiencing Sophia so powerfully, I was filled with an evangelical zeal to tell the good news about Sophia wherever and whenever I could. I preached it in church, I told the story to friends, I studied more myself and wrote books with two friends, I gathered people together for study and prayer, I gave workshops. There was a great release of energy and creativity that spread to several circles of friends and colleagues. Sophia's creative energy enlivened many, women and men. But it has been among women where her presence has made a powerful difference.

Sophia affirmed my identity as a woman in all aspects of my being, and she has done the same for many other women. Her divine female power is readily available, affirming me and others at the most fundamental level of our being: our bodies. The change that happened in my body when she appeared in the moment of that vision so many years ago has never left, no matter how difficult the circumstances.

I have witnessed Sophia's extraordinary power working in women's lives. I've seen women who had been sexually abused as children or who have been raped find healing at remarkable depths through her; her power has touched them in their bodies where they have been violated. I've encountered women whose strong identity was made even stronger. I think of a 70-year-old Roman Catholic nun, a nurse working among the poor in Brooklyn, who announced, "I've been trying to be Jesus for the people all my life — his hands, his feet, his voice — but I am Sophia for the people. It just fits." Sophia's hands, Sophia's feet, Sophia's voice — Sophia's body in its splendid femaleness, Sophia's divine power embodied in women who claim her power — this is the most powerful aspect of knowing her.

I've experienced the affirmation women receive as they know Sophia not only as divine female but also as the creative one with whom they can identify. She took part in creation (Prov. 8:22-31); she built a house and cooked a banquet (Prov. 9:1-6); she is called the "mother" of "all good things" (Wisdom 7:11-12); and she continues to be a part of the creative process of humanity (Sirach 1:14). She invites a deep identification with her among women in their giving birth and mothering, gardening and cooking, building houses and creating rituals — in a whole variety of creative enterprises. She's the source of creative energy for artists among us. She's inspired poetry, drama, songs, dances, and a variety of art works, often with a deep sense of her powerful presence in the process.

Friends of mine, professors teaching at the graduate level of universities, have been especially drawn to her as Wisdom, both female and knowledge, because she affirms both their female bodies and their intellects. They keep reminding me that Sophia means

Wisdom; she's learning and intellectual endeavor. As "Wisdom, the fashioner of all things," she is the one who teaches the sciences, from "the structure of the world" to "the varieties of plants and the virtues of roots" (Wisdom 7:17-22). She is "the mistress of the art of thought" in Proverbs 8:12, NJB. As Divine Wisdom, she is available to women in all endeavors of learning, from music theory to molecular biology. I've found her powerfully present in the midst of the unfolding mysteries of the universe the physicists are showing us. What an important model for women's own intellectual growth, for our teaching and our learning, as she heals the mind/body split!

When we gather, we women cherish the opportunity to share our stories. Sophia affirms this aspect of our life together in the powerful way she tells her own story. She "praises herself and tells of her glory in the midst of her people" (Sirach 24:1). It is incredibly powerful when women not only tell their stories but also name their gifts out loud, singing their own praises in the assembly of sisters. As women learn to take pride in ourselves and in one another, to shed feelings of inadequacy, to stand tall and proud as deserving of respect in all arenas of our lives, I am aware of Sophia's power living in us in new, strong ways.

Sophia's assertiveness has been an important model for change in me, for I tend to be quiet and agreeable even when it's not in my best interest. Her words in Proverbs:

> To you, O people, I call,
>   and my cry is to all that live. . . .
> Hear, for I will speak noble things,
>   and from my lips will come what is right. (Prov. 8:4,6)

have been important in helping me find my own words to focus energy for change. I've invited women to follow Sophia's lead in demanding the attention we deserve, in speaking out insistently on our own behalf, in claiming anger as a powerful means of opening energy for change. One woman I worked with who had been abused as a child found her voice in poetry that spoke of her rage and pain as well as of her healing. Sophia's strong demanding presence helped her spit out the ugliness of her experiences, filling her with new creative energy and assurance.

Most importantly, I've experienced how Sophia empowers me and other women as we assume leadership — leadership in the church as well as in every other aspect of society. Her power enables rulers to exercise their leadership justly:

> *By me monarchs rule*
>   *and princes decree what is right;*
> *by me rulers govern,*
>   *so do nobles, the lawful authorities.* (Prov. 8:15-16, NJB)

She is a wonderfully fitting model for women who would lead. I experience Sophia's divine power whenever I see my clergy sisters stepping out into new arenas of leadership within the church, whether it be as pastor of a large and challenging congregation, as a district superintendent, or as a bishop — not doing the job in the old ways but creatively using their own experiences and insights as women to bring something new. We women are claiming our own authority in a way that helps the church grow.

I believe that with Sophia as an important part of the Godhead, women's inferior status in the church will begin to change. I hope for the day when the church will proudly lift up Sophia as divine symbol, contributing to equalizing relations between the sexes at all levels of society.

Controversy in the Church

Living with Sophia, celebrating her presence in me and in all aspects of life, has in the meantime led to some very rough times in the church. The past four years have been full of controversy within The United Methodist Church, much of it focusing on me. Letters have been circulated to all of the United Methodist churches in eastern Pennsylvania and articles have been written in national denominational publications accusing me of all manner of things. I have been accused of being a witch, a pagan, the anti-Christ, a heretic, a man-hating lesbian, and a prostitute for a goddess cult.

Resolutions appear every year at our annual meeting, denouncing the Sophia "heresy" and often calling for my censure or removal, along with that of Hal Taussig, my colleague in ministry and my co-author of books on Sophia. The controversy even spawned a new organization in our region, the "Jesus Christ Is Lord Task Force," aimed at fighting the threat of feminism, especially as articulated in "the Sophia heresy." My interest in and enthusiasm for spreading the word about Sophia ran right into a virulent backlash resulting from the fear of the growing power of women in the church and the changes we are bringing.

It has been a terribly difficult time for me. I wish I could say that I stood strong through it all, that at every moment I felt Sophia's strength undergirding me. Not so. There were times, especially during the first year of controversy, when I came close to breaking. The irony of my earlier experience of Sophia having kept me in the church only to get dragged through such abuse later seemed like a cruel joke. On my worst days, it felt as though she were punishing me. On other days I began to understand better the passages about her demanding and difficult ways:

> *She seems very harsh to the undisciplined;*
> *   fools cannot remain with her.*
> *She will be like a heavy stone to test them,*
> *   and they will not delay in casting her aside.*
> *For Wisdom is like her name;*
> *   she is not readily perceived by many.* (Sirach 6:20-22)

At the same time, there were other ways that I experienced Sophia during that period that helped me survive and grow. I remember one particularly difficult period, when in addition to fielding the various insults being hurled my way, I continued to pastor my congregation, wend my way through a divorce while parenting my two children and dealing with the death of my father. During this time I went on spiritual retreat to revive my sagging spirits. The spiritual director took one look at me, said I looked very depleted, gave me Psalm 131 to pray before retiring, and suggested

I go to bed. One line from that psalm I repeated over and over to myself, like a mantra: "I hold myself in quiet and silence, like a child in its mother's arms" (Ps. 131:2, NJB). As I lay in bed, repeating that line, changing it to "like a child in my mother's arms," it was as if the bed were Sophia's arms and lap, and I was snuggled in, safely held, and loved. This was a new side of Sophia for me; not only did she challenge me to move forward in new ways when that was what I needed, but she was there to hold me when I needed to retreat and lick my wounds.

There was another way Sophia supported me during this time; she helped me find my anger. I'm a person who has always had difficulty with conflict; fighting never came easily. The anger that was rightfully mine was buried so deep that I didn't even know it was there, but it sapped my energy and my spirit. Close friends kept asking me why I wasn't angry. They kept urging me to speak up. My therapist, too, offered the opinion that there must be as much rage inside me as there was being directed at me. It took me a long time to find it, but the constant nudging by so many seemed to be Sophia working through my friends to emulate her own passionate anger at those who rejected her: "I also will laugh at your calamity; I will mock when panic strikes you" (Prov. 1:26). I practiced shouting that text out loud, privately railing at my accusers, adding my own words. Later I gathered my anger, using it to speak from the pulpit, organize educational sessions at church gatherings, write letters rebuffing my attackers, and a variety of other things. Today, attacks still come from time to time, but my anger is there, ready to energize me to respond with strength and confidence. Conflict is still difficult for me, I wish it would go away, but Sophia has led me right into the thick of it. The fundamental changes that she symbolizes will of necessity bring conflict. I'm learning to live with it and to use it.

Opportunity for Change

I have been encouraged in the midst of the conflict by a growing number of women and men in the church who are finding important connections to Sophia in their own lives. Seeing the changes that knowing her makes for others makes the struggle worthwhile. A clergyman came up to me privately, early on in the controversy, and shared that both he and his wife had been abused by their fathers as children; male God imagery was extremely painful to them both. Because his story was very private, he couldn't speak about it in the larger gathering; even so, he sought me out to let me know the issue was important. I recall two laywomen coming up to me at the end of our annual conference, women I'd never met before or since, who thanked me for staying in the church. One woman timidly spoke up at a church gathering in which most people were angry and hostile to me and to thinking of God in feminine terms. She had been praying to Divine Wisdom for years because she seemed so much more accessible; yet she always had somehow felt guilty. She wept quietly as she offered her gratitude that someone would bring Sophia out in the open for everyone. I have countless more stories like that. It is people like these, ordinary people whose lives are being opened to new possibilities within the church because of Sophia's presence, that make staying in the church worthwhile.

Sophia is bringing important changes to the church. She is becoming a symbol for the growth of women's power. More and more women within the church are finding their own voices and speaking them. Women are exercising leadership on all levels of church life with new creativity and power, with confidence that their dreams and visions, their unique spiritual gifts are important to lift up. The hostile reaction in this controversy underscores just how significant the changes are. The controversy only simmered while I served a small church with little status. Several laypeople sought to stir up trouble but without much success. It was only upon my appointment, by a woman bishop, to a prestigious downtown church, that the controversy was unleashed with incredible venom. At that point, male clergy joined the fray, keeping the controversy fueled and focused. The strength of the reaction is in direct proportion to the strength of the changes taking place within the church. The conflict itself is a sign of Sophia's growing power and the power in women.

Sophia will not go away. She is within the biblical tradition and within the larger Christian tradition. She offers the church divine female presence that cannot be ignored. She cannot be read out of the Bible; neither can the experience of a growing number of church people who find her important be easily dismissed. Women are coming into the center of church life, and Sophia is emerging again in our time in direct correlation to the power that women have to shape church life. Sophia offers the church the opportunity for inclusive God language and imagery that affirms women's full personhood and widens men's spiritual possibilities. Sophia is part of our tradition, even as I and women like me are a part of the church. We always have been. The church, and the women and men in it hoping for change, are too important to stop the struggle now. Sophia kept me in the church, Sophia got me into the struggle, and Sophia still is the reason for staying. She is a powerful divine presence in our midst; she leads us all into an open future.

Susan Cole

Chapter 16

SPIRITUALITY IS ABOUT SURVIVAL

Marie M. Fortune

Marie M. Fortune, M.Div., is the executive director of the Center for the Prevention of Sexual and Domestic Violence, Seattle, Washington. This educational ministry serves as a training resource to religious communities in the United States and Canada. Marie grew up in North Carolina and was ordained a minister in the United Church of Christ in 1976. She is the author of numerous books, including *Clergy Misconduct: Sexual Abuse in the Ministerial Relationship* (with Deborah Woolley, et al., 1992), *Is Nothing Sacred? When Sex Invades the Pastoral Relationship* (1989), *Keeping the Faith: Questions and Answers for Abused Women* (1987), and *Sexual Violence: The Unmentionable Sin* (1983). To temper the demands of her work, Marie delights in "tomatoes and grits, dogs and baseball."

I do not know how to write *about* spirituality. Rather like a poem or song, spirituality is something to be experienced, momentarily instructive and never definitive. I do know how to study and pray, watch and listen, exercise and play, and I thereby receive the resources that sustain my spirit. As long as I am able to maintain these disciplines of prayer, study, watchfulness, and recreation, I have what for me provides courage in the face of evil, strength in the face of suffering, and thanksgiving in the face of joy. My survival depends on courage, strength, and joy. At its most basic, I believe that spirituality is about survival: It is what gets us through each day.

Known, Loved, Accountable

A number of years ago, my spiritual director asked me this question: "What do you know about your relationship with God?" The answer came fairly quickly — at least I articulated it quickly — although it required further reflection: I know that I am *known*, I am *loved*, and I am *accountable to my sisters*.

This relationship with a God who lives within and among us is both corporate and individual. I know that I am fully known and fully loved by God. There are no secrets here. God knows my confusion and my clarity, my hesitation and my assertiveness, my fatigue and my faithfulness, my struggles and my victories. "Where can I go from your spirit? Where can I flee from your presence?" (Ps. 139:7).

Because God knows me, God loves me. I am loved not because of who I am or in spite of who I am but simply because I am. There is nothing that can separate me from God's love — not a homophobic church, not a woman-hating culture, not rejection by those who do not understand, not my failings or shortcomings. This love that passes my understanding is the essence of God's grace and God's gift of creation.

Because from those to whom much has been given, much is expected, I am responsible to use my gifts. As I was raised up in the community of God's faithful people, where God lives and moves and has her being, both my faith and my awareness were nurtured. Sometimes this community of the faithful gathers in a church; often it gathers elsewhere. Within church and without, those who taught me helped me understand who I am as a woman and how my life is dependent upon my relationships with my sisters. In these relationships, I am accountable to use what resources I have to learn from the African American poet and the Korean theologian, to advocate for the Filipina immigrant, to stand beside the victim of rape, to speak for those silenced by violence and abuse, to listen to the wisdom of the older woman, to hear the challenge of the Jewish woman, to stand together with other lesbian women. It is my faith tradition that requires that in these relationships, I always seek to make justice real among us.

Who is the God who knows and loves and calls us to accountability? She is the God described in Hebrew and Christian Scripture as a pillar of fire, a shepherd, a mother hen, a woman giving birth. She is my source, my shield, my song who provides all that I need. In the words of Bobby McFerrin's "The 23rd Psalm":

> Even though I walk, through a dark and dreary land,
>   There is nothing that can shake me,
> She has said she won't forsake me,
>   I'm in her hand.[1]

A Dark and Dreary Land

And who am I in this place and time? As a woman who is Anglo, middle-class, lesbian, and Christian, born and raised in the southeastern United States, I know that every day I walk "through a dark and dreary land."

I know what it means to be female in a patriarchal world. As a woman, the smell and taste of woman-hating greet me every morning. Misogyny pollutes the air I breathe. From newspaper headlines of another woman sentenced for self-defense against some man's violence, to morning radio describing the latest case of child sexual abuse by a priest, from the billboard advertising "Girls, Girls, Girls" at the local topless club to the music lyrics testifying that women are bitches and love to be hit, from the news of Bosnian women being systematically raped and tortured by soldiers to another Hollywood film portraying women as evil and/or victims, from the catcalls on the street to the overheard conversation in the grocery line of a husband telling his wife that she'll be sorry when they get home, the constancy of woman-hating almost convinces me that it is normal. Every day I hear the stories of men's violence toward women and children, of hate crimes toward people of color, Jews, gays, and lesbians, and every day I turn around and this evil is staring me in the face. I see and hear evil in rape, domestic violence, incest, ritual abuse, and sexual harassment. It is the price women and children pay for being in this world at this time.

I know how it feels to be marginal and vulnerable to this evil. Every day I accommodate my life to it: The doors of my home are always locked. I always have to consider the risk when I encounter two or more men on the street. The dog barking or a knock on the door always first means danger. Working late alone always means figuring out security options. The raised voice of a male colleague in a committee meeting usually means negative consequences sooner or later. The constant reality of vulnerability because I am female and physically small brings fear and anger. Both fear and anger are instructive; both make for survival. I try to pay attention to both. Fear alerts me to very real dangers; anger moves me to act for myself and others. I am thankful for both.

But the evil that they indicate, sharp and cold as a knifeblade, is also complicated as it lives and moves within and among us. Evil is not always so apparent, so clear; it is also subtle and can come wearing a smiling, charming face. Evil is institutionalized in seemingly reasonable words on paper whose real purpose is to protect sexual predators from consequences rather than protect those whom they would victimize. Evil is played out as savage ignorance by those who choose not to know and to pass by on the other side.

The evil of woman-hating is the most salient reminder to me that I am a stranger here.

> *By the rivers of Babylon —*
> *there we sat down and there we wept*
> *when we remembered Zion.*

On the willow there
*   we hung up our harps.*
For there our captors
*   asked us for songs,*
and our tormentors asked for mirth, saying,
*   "Sing us one of the songs of Zion!"*

How can we sing [God's] song
*   in a foreign land?* (Ps. 137:1-4)

How, indeed?

And how can one know a just and merciful God in the midst of genocide, rape, domestic violence, ritual abuse, incest, and the Holocaust? This is the very place I look for God, present in the midst of suffering, offering the courage and strength necessary for resistance.

There is nothing that can shake me,
*   She has said she won't forsake me,*
I'm in her hand.[2]

Most of the time I know this; some of the time I wonder. But I do know that if spirituality does not speak to the presence of evil, it is of no use to women. For me, spirituality does not offer platitudes or pretense but rather a way to comprehend what makes for my survival. My spirituality has to include a recognition of the reality of evil and specifically of violence against women. If it does not, it is only a facade that supports the collective denial of this reality and as such, it is not only inadequate, it is also dangerous to me. But if I can name what I know spiritually, then I can also look to spiritual resources to help me deal with it.

Then the overriding question is: Is there a possibility that justice may roll down like water when what we know is a parched and barren place? Is there a respite from "this dark and dreary land"? Is there a response to this evil among us? Perhaps this is the meaning of faith:

> *Faith is the assurance of things hoped for, the conviction of things not seen. . . . All of these died in faith without having received the promises, but from a distance, they saw and greeted them. They confessed that they were strangers and foreigners on the earth, for people who speak in this way make it clear that they are seeking a homeland.* (Heb. 11:1, 13-14)

This is a promise I can live with. It would be hard to live without it.

The Temptations of Privilege

But then I also live with the particularity of being Anglo, middle-class, Christian, and a U.S. citizen. And as such I know what it means to have access to privilege in the midst of an excess of need. My spirituality must also address this reality. I live with the paradox of privilege and marginality at the same time. There is no time for guilt or despair about this fact; there is also no need for sympathy. But there is a need for careful, responsible use of whatever resources are mine in order to bring those who are marginal to the center and lessen the impact of privilege, to seek justice and reparations for the horrors of our shared histories. Of course I could pretend not to notice: This is the prerogative of privilege. In my whiteness, my Christianity, and my citizenship, I could walk away from knowing. But she will not let me hide "face down in ignorance," as Maya Angelou writes in "On the Pulse of the Morning."[3] It is

> *amazing grace, how sweet the sound,*
> *   that saved a wretch like me.*
> *I once was lost, but now am found,*
> *   was blind but now I see*

according to the words of John Newton, the slave-ship captain who wrote this hymn.

But the temptations are there nonetheless. I am tempted constantly by passivity, by silence, by cynicism, by ignorance. I am tempted by privilege that says come stand here with us and we will save you from the demands of the have-nots. Come, pretend not to know what you know, and you will be safe. Come, forget what you have learned, and they will leave you alone. Come, say nothing, and they will not notice that you are here. Come, close your eyes, and you will not feel despair. Come, do as you are told, and you will be rewarded.

But Audre Lorde taught me that my silence will not protect me. Frances Wood taught me that I can't not know what I know. Maya Angelou taught me that I may stand upon the rock but must not hide my face in its shadow. Alice Walker taught me that I am not the first "to suffer, rebel, fight, love and die." Vaclav Havel taught me that hope is not the belief that we can change things; hope is the conviction that what we do matters. Lee Tai-Young, the first woman lawyer in Korea, challenged me to "do something no one else can do, or what no one else is doing. Do something for justice."[4]

So I have learned that I will survive only with eyes and ears wide open, and in solidarity with those who seek to do justice, love kindness, and walk humbly with God (Micah 6:8) regardless of race, class, gender, nationality, sexual orientation, or religious affiliation.

Of course resisting the temptation of ignorance means accepting the burden of knowledge. Then I am faced with two choices: to sink into despair because I know too much about the evil that lives in my church, in my neighborhood, in my country, or to look evil in the eye from a place of hope and act upon it. This hope is anything but denial dressed in pretty flowers. It is the hope that comes from the Spirit that dwells within and among us.

Present — and Listening

This Spirit calls us to action in ministry. But sometimes, doing becomes the temptation. In the face of innumerable victims of violence and abuse whose needs for compassion, justice, and resources are overwhelming, I am tempted to run faster: Good works will bring justice and healing. I will write another book, make another speech, return another call. While my efforts are useful, I must not presume that my efforts alone will suffice. Perhaps there are times when there is nothing I can do. I must also be able to wait, listen, stand by.

In *The Oath*, Elie Wiesel describes a reluctant rabbi who replies to this question from his student: "What am I to do? Advise me, guide me. The night ahead of me is black and dense, it opens unto horror and ashes. Where do I fit in? What is my duty? To whom do I owe allegiance?" The rabbi replies:

> *I warn you: I am not, nor shall I be, a maker of miracles or a dispenser of indulgences. Don't look upon me as a substitute for study or prayer or as a mediator between you and heaven. If you are seeking someone to lighten your task of being a Jew, then look elsewhere. Easy solutions are not my way. I warn you: I shall not tell you what to do, nor shall I tell you which goals are desirable and which are not; I shall not give orders nor shall I provide remedies. All I promise is to be present. And listen.*[5]

Perhaps as a minister, this is all I can promise as well.

Guarding the Good Treasure

What do I know with certainty? I know that the body apart from the spirit is dead, that faith apart from works is dead, and that peace apart from justice is deadly. If I am to survive and be of any use, it is my task to bring these parts together and hold them in tension.

Finally I know that it is only in the dailiness of life that I live and move and have my being. It is the tangible, sensual manifestations of the Spirit that give me sustenance for my vocation: the shared laughter at absurdity, the photograph that makes one's mouth water, the softness of salt water and easy current of the surf, the reassuring touch of a life partner who knows so much, the taste of salmon baked over fire and fresh basil pesto spread over hot polenta, the rich sweetness of a tuberose, the dry bite of a chardonnay, the warmth of my dog's fur and the rough wetness of her tongue, the stretch of a cat's body, the crack of a homerun, the grace of a no-hitter, the explosive power of lava flowing into the sea, the softness of my mother's cheek, the hymn that brings the word so long stifled, the satisfaction of a job done well, the tears that flow when justice is manifest even in its brevity, the bread and wine shared in a faithful community, the affirmation when truth is finally spoken, never complete, but truth nonetheless, the quiet in the city covered by fresh snow, the joy in the child who has learned to read, the smell of a tomato just pulled from the vine sliced and laid next to green beans simmered all day with fatback and a side of garlic-cheese grits, the waiting quietly for death to come to one loved for so long, her hand in mine, not afraid, just waiting. In these moments of the ordinary and mundane, I know that "I am in her hand."

So I understand and paraphrase Paul's words to Timothy:

> I am reminded of your sincere faith, a faith that lived first in your grandmother Marie Marshall and your mother Lina Hendley and now, I am sure, lives in you. For this reason I remind you to rekindle the gift of God that is within you through the laying on of hands; for God did not give us a spirit of cowardice, but rather a spirit of power and of love and of self-discipline. . . . Guard the good treasure entrusted to you. (2 Tim. 1:5-7, 14)

What more can I do but guard the good treasure that has been entrusted to me?

Chapter 17

ON THE VERGE OF GIVING BIRTH

Carmen Guerrero

Carmen Guerrero, D.D., is the Hispanic missioner in the Episcopal Diocese of Los Angeles. After her ordination in January 1985, she worked in Honduras for four years coordinating a theological education program to raise a Honduran priesthood. She later served a parish in West Texas. In addition to leadership development of Hispanic lay people, Carmen devotes great energy to her work as preacher, speaker, and retreat director at spirituality formation events and as a keynoter at conferences on justice issues such as immigration, AIDS, violence against women, and racism. She is an associate of the Community of Saint Mary, Southern Province, and lives at Casa Santa Maria, a convent recently opened in inner city Los Angeles.

A woman who "could not be healed by anyone" dared to touch the fringe of Jesus' garment. That was about 2,000 years ago.

An African American woman who had not attended a "formal seminary" dared to be nominated for bishop in a church that had no women bishops. That was over five years ago.

And I was present when three modern churchwomen — that same African American bishop, the Right Reverend Barbara Harris; a white American seminary dean, Dr. Mary June Nestler; and a Korean theologian, Dr. Chung Hyun Kyung — together dared to dream new dreams and dissolve images. That was last year.

Since that gathering at an Episcopal Church Women's conference, I have been involved in a wonderful inner struggle, sometimes with a feeling of chaos, sometimes being able to see quite clearly, sometimes angry, sometimes in pain, and many times full of anticipation and expectation.

The sources of this inner struggle have been primarily these women — one from the distant past and the others in the midst of the church today. Their words and their behavior have led me to question everything that I have ever been taught about the Christian faith. Oh, not that I have lost it, but that I am calling it into question. I'm holding Christianity and all its teachings accountable. And I have a sense of being on the verge of giving birth, of bringing forth new life.

Much of what I write here has been called up by the voices of these women — the fringe-touching woman, the new bishop, the seminary dean, the theologian, and the many others who have touched my life before them but who somehow were only voices in the distance. Most dramatically, the voices of women sharing their stories of horrible violence and suffering now resound in my mind and cry out in direct contradiction to what the church has always taught about suffering: that suffering is something about which a good Christian should rejoice.

The voices blend together at times, but occasionally I can hear something distinct that guides my own response. I can hear Bishop Barbara Harris's voice at the conference saying: "God is calling us as women to something new. This new calling requires an ability to see into the future, not blindly and as an escape from the present, but in order to envision what can and must be — if we are to be the prophets who speak God's word."

Being futuristic, however, is not possible in a vacuum. It must be connected with our past, and it must be connected with the richness of the spirituality of our foremothers.

Why our foremothers? Why not our forefathers? Aren't our forefathers what the church has always taught us to hear? Could it be that it is *precisely* that patriarchal spirituality of our forefathers that has led us to the reality in which we exist today? That reality of life in which we have missed the mark of our purpose for being on this planet and in this universe? We have lost the sense of holiness in all things and people and nothing seems worth the struggle for justice.

Therefore, the call must be to look toward the future, drawing from the depths of what our foremothers have so richly given us. We would not have survived this long were it not for the remnant of our mothers' spirituality that lives in every woman.

Does God Change?

But what is this spirituality? According to Matthew Fox, being spiritual is being alive, being filled with Ruach, breathing deeply, being in touch with the wind.[1] A sense of female spirituality is very upsetting to a church, a society, a world that predominantly sees through traditional patriarchal eyes, that imagines God to be one who is immutable, unchanging. To revision that God also involves revisioning ourselves as women created in the image of God.

Walter Brueggmann, in his book *Hopeful Imagination*, writes about "statements of hope and new possibility" that help "people in exile to receive the newness of God and act on the new ... possibilities now being made available."[2] When the image of God is one of immutability and the image of woman is one of continuous change, how then are we as women to fathom being made in the image of God?

At that same conference, Korean theologian Chung Hyun Kyung encouraged us as women to stop to think about it: Women are always changing, much like the wind. When boys grow, they simply become bigger; they basically have the same body parts, only bigger. When girls grow, they develop new parts they never had before. Their breasts become full, their hips widen, their menstrual cycle begins, they produce eggs that can be fertilized and produce new life. If they become pregnant, their bellies swell, and after they give birth, their bellies flatten out again. How can a woman be created in the image of God when she is always changing and God never changes? Either she is not created in the image of God or our understanding of God needs to be challenged. For me, this is all very disconcerting because I have always believed in an immutable, unchanging God. And I have taught this to others.

But now I must ask, does God change? If God doesn't change, then what about prayer? What about the parables of Jesus such as the woman who persists until she changes the mind of the unjust judge (Luke 18:1-8)? What about the preaching of the prophets? What about forgiveness? Do these not suggest the image of a God whose mind changes?

A New Vision

I am convinced that we *are* called to envision a new way of understanding God and a new way of reading Scriptures that in the past have been interpreted in such a way that the very word of God that one would hope could bring life and liberation in effect has brought death and oppression.

When I listen to the voice of the woman from the distant past, the Jewish woman who had been hemorrhaging for twelve years, her voice inspires me also to say to the religious institutions of our times, "No, do not do this to me. This cannot be right before God." Her actions inspire me to dare a new vision of God.

Luke 8:43-48 tells us about the woman who came up behind Jesus and touched the fringe of his clothes. The religious system of the time in which this woman lived taught her that whoever even *touches* anything that she has touched is unclean. In Leviticus, the Book of the Law, the book of the religious establishment, we read:

"Who ever touches [a woman with a discharge of blood] shall be unclean. Everything upon which she lies shall be unclean; everything also upon which she sits shall be unclean. All the days of the discharge she shall continue in uncleanness" (Lev. 15:19-20, 25). Said another way, this woman embodied uncleanness. She was untouchable. And she had been the embodiment of this "uncleanness" for twelve years. This meant no human contact, no human touch. It meant total separation, it meant exile, and it was all sanctioned by the very religious institution that believed itself to be in relationship with God.

Jesus, on the way to heal the daughter of Jairus, has now been defiled by this woman's touch; he senses something different has happened in him and in that crowd pressing around him.

"Who touched me?"

All denied it, including the woman. Twelve years of suffering had silenced her voice.

Peter said, "Everyone! The crowds pressed in on you. . . ."

Jesus rebutted him: "No, this was different. Someone touched me. I noticed that power went out of me."

Listen to this! A sick, unclean woman touches the incarnate God, and power is released! Her touch evokes a response from Jesus. And the woman comes forward, trembling, falling down before him. *She* knew the seriousness of her actions. The people around her knew the seriousness of her actions. And Jesus, a Jewish man, knew the seriousness of her daring touch. Without the daring, the healing would have been impossible. And the religious teaching of her day almost triumphed.

We can console ourselves naively and say, "Thank goodness, we don't live in those times." But to do that is to ignore our own acceptance of interpretations of Scripture in connection with suffering. Have we not come to fully accept that suffering is a virtue for which we must thank God?

There was a story in *The New York Times* recently about a woman in Bosnia who was raped repeatedly for a whole day by several armed men, and she never made a sound, never cried out, never lifted her voice.

It was her little baby girl who sat on the floor next to her while she was being raped who screamed and cried during the whole ordeal. Finally, one of the men picked up the little girl by the hair, cut off her head, and threw it at the woman. It was then that the woman got up and ran through the village with her child's head in her hands, screaming for her child.

There is a suffering in this world that is not from God and yet our interpretation of Scripture does not seem to allow for this. Either we have a very sick religion and a very sick God, or we have not even begun to know how to interpret God's Word.

That is what the story of the woman in Luke's Gospel is about — someone who dared to say to the religious institution of her time, "No, God *can* touch me, God *can* heal me, God *can* give new meaning to my life, regardless of what the church has said about God. This woman with no name, this woman who is all women, dared to raise her voice in the streets: She dared to say No! She dared to declare justice for all the untouchable. She dared to ask questions of her religion and dared to hold it accountable. Basically she dared to envision that God is much more than the definitions religious institutions can provide.

And to this daring act, Jesus, God Incarnate, responds by saying, "Daughter, your faith has made you well" (Luke 8:48).

A New Faith

What kind of faith is this? It has gone against the established rule of the institution that had already defined this woman's role in society.

I believe this is a new kind of faith. It is a faith that comes from knowing and trusting that there is a future. It is a faith that can envision God acting in a different way.

This woman's faith is every woman's faith. Through her faith she dared to reach out, hoping against hope that God was different from what she had been taught, believing in a God who would indeed acknowledge the untouchable and include them in the family of God. She dared to let her voice be heard.

As women who know there is a future, who know life has to be different, we need to let our voices be heard. But how can they be heard if they are not even raised? How can our words ring out for justice if we cannot even make the sounds, if we cannot envision a new image of who we are, based on a new image of who God is?

How can we stop the injustice of a world that is on a path to self-destruction: destruction of animals, destruction of plants, destruction of the air we breathe, destruction of children and men, and most importantly for us, destruction of women, of the life-givers of this society?

Why are we not at the places where decisions of justice are made? I know why I have not been. I have believed the interpretations of others. I have accepted what my fathers, my brothers, my sons, my husbands have taught me about who I am and what I am worth, and who God is. I never questioned it. I only believed it and accepted it. I dismissed as erroneous, as ill-informed, as lies, as perhaps heresy, the voices of my sisters, my wives, my daughters, and my mothers.

And now I want to cry, I want to wail, I want to lament the loss. I am convinced that the very God of the universe is calling us to cry out in the street, the market place, where we work, where we worship, where we live — calling us to raise our voices where decisions of justice are made.

Can we dare to do any less?

Can we dare to challenge what we have been so willing to accept without question even when it negated our very being? Bishop Barbara Harris challenges women to dare to look into the future, anchored in the spirituality of our mothers, and envision a new way of being God's people in the world.

May we have the courage to dream dreams about a faith that can make us well because we have dared to have a new vision of who God is.

Carmen B. Guerrero

SECTION FIVE

THEOLOGIANS

"But when Priscilla and Aquila heard him, they took him aside and explained the Way of God to him more accurately."

Acts 18:26

Chapter 18

RADICAL TRUST

Anne Clarke Brown

Anne Clarke Brown, M.S., M.A., is a candidate for the degree doctor of theology in Anglican studies at The General Theological Seminary (Episcopal) in New York City, where she has also taught Greek and women's spirituality. One of her ministries as part of the laity is spiritual direction. In her former life as an urban planner, Anne managed historic restoration projects in San Antonio, Texas. She is now developing her own construction skills by building a timber-frame house in Vermont. Sixty-six of her architectural photographs have been published in *Rockefeller Center: Architecture as Theatre* (1978), edited by Alan Balfour.

Rooted in Connection

 T he rain this afternoon is perfect metal-roof rain: heavy down-pours coming in waves with periods of gentler rain between, then dripping from the trees, occasionally intensified by a breeze through the leaves. I am dry inside, and yet the metal roof communicates the rain, connects me to the doings outside this small house a friend and I are building in Vermont. For me, attention to such communication is essential to my commitment to try always to live with care. So, I come to this small house and its metal roof to find grounding, rootedness in the many connections of my life, and to learn to dwell in their depths.

My friend Lee and I bought the land in June of 1992. We decided to begin our building with what later will be an addition — an L-shaped main room and a bathroom, with a loft above the bath and part of the main room. "Continuous architecture" is a term used to describe the rural New England houses that have a series of additions attached to one end of the main building, often culminating with a barn. Because we could not afford to build a complete house, ours is continuous architecture in reverse. Although there will be no barn, the house proper will be built last.

The view from the house is of an intimate sort — aspen, birch, and maple trees on a fern-covered slope, a small pond at the bottom with forest beyond. A mountain ridge visible just above the treetops hints of a larger world, but today it is hidden in clouds. I was drawn to this site over others with more spacious views, and I am only beginning to understand why. I am not ready to live constantly with the awesomeness of the spectacular, where so much is revealed at once. I can delight in several such prospects a short walk from the door, but I need to spend time with the particularities of smaller bits of life — the lone columbine blooming among the ferns, hoof prints of deer near the pond, bulging burls on the trunk of a sweet birch — particularities that emerge as one becomes intimate with a landscape. A perceptive friend who came to offer a few days of work on the house must have known this even before I was able to articulate it, for she cajoled the young man running the excavator into placing a large "sitting rock" just below the house. It has become a favorite place for contemplation and prayer (in non-bug season!). We call the rock by our friend's name.

I was able to spend the summer of 1992 — the rainiest Vermont has seen in many years — living in a tent and working on the house. The manual work was a more-than-welcome respite from four solid years of academic study (I am working on a doctorate in theology) and part-time teaching in an Episcopal seminary. We hired local contractors for the excavation, foundation walls, timber frame, exterior walls, and roof. We are doing the rest — installation of windows and doors, clapboard siding, interior walls, insulation, plumbing, wiring, flooring, and painting — ourselves. The work is slow, for we have much to learn as we go, but rewarding in its permanent results, results that reflect our own loving care. Here, too, attention is needed, the attention in which hours can pass unnoticed while one is absorbed in a task. Such self-forgetful working is itself a form of deep connectedness, of prayer.

The most remarkable, and indeed the most surprising, aspect of the building experience was the people who came to work on the house and from whom we bought materials. They were, with one exception, all men. Experience had led me to expect at least some of the condescending treatment often directed at women who stray into traditionally male activities. I remember buying a luggage carrier for my bicycle in New York. The young man at the cash register informed me that they could not put it on the bicycle for me that day. I said I had planned to put it on myself, and he replied, "You're going to put it on? You need tools, you know." I said not to worry and left him with a "Yeah, sure, lady" look on his face. More recently, in quite different circumstances but arising out of the same need to trivialize and diminish, I had been told that a course I proposed on the practical implications of feminist theory and theology for ministry and the church was deemed inappropriate for the institution in which I hoped to offer it. But these Vermont men were different. I heard not one patronizing or condescending remark all summer. Instead, they assumed that I knew what I was doing. If I asked for advice, we would puzzle through the problem together. They did their own work with care and trusted that others would do the same.

Starting in Trust

Trust. I did not need any of the rejoinders one fantasizes about using in response to sexist comments — or wishes one had made if only one had thought quickly enough. Instead, I needed to relearn trust, trust not only in others but also in myself and in God. When I worked for a large building contractor, part of my job was the preparation and negotiation of contracts in which the responsibilities of all parties were carefully outlined. Instinct, however, told both Lee and me that trust would be the foundation for our small house, and we did not request, nor did any of our contractors request, written agreements. We discussed what needed doing, they told us what they thought it would cost, they did the work, and we paid them. As I reflect on the process, I can picture many of the men I have known and worked with in the past shaking their heads and rolling their eyes at our naïveté. But I realize that what began as an intuitive response became a conscious decision that went beyond naïveté. We chose radical trust rather than fear as the starting point of our working relationships.

Had fear been our starting point — as I believe it is for many human interactions — we would have been concerned only with how we would be affected by a relationship, particularly with how we might be hurt or wronged. We might have said, "If we give Joe money in advance for materials, how do we know he won't disappear or cheat on the quality and pocket the difference?" Our goal would have been to diminish our risk by gaining greater control over Joe and his work. The irony, of course, is that we can never truly control what we fear, for fear objectifies what is feared, and our fear of that object, that other, then has control of us.

Guided by trust, we are open to others, willing to engage with them in a spirit of mutuality and respect rather than one of suspicion and fear. Trust is a form of hospitality that allows us to welcome and come to know those who are different, and it allows us to recognize that we, too, are Other to others. By using the term "radical" trust, I mean to emphasize the conscious intentionality in which such trust is founded. Radical trust is essential to the formation and continued vitality of our human communities, for trust is the way through which the common ground of community is revealed and maintained. By following the way of trust, we also discover the common ground we share with the natural world around us. We comprehend our place as part — not ruler or beneficiary — of the interconnected, interdependent web of creation.

Living with Care

As a Christian, I see radical trust as an aspect of the Love that moves out to embrace the world from the heart of the gospel. Radical trust is the active response of faith to the gift of divine love. It is a way of living with care, a way of acting out of the strength of love rather than out of the weakness of fear. Whereas fear turns me in upon myself, forces me into the language of duality, of "either/or" choices, of exclusion, trust draws me toward what I call life at the edge, the territory of paradox and ambiguity. Fear does not somehow miraculously disappear, but the practice of trust deprives fear of its power to control. The paradoxical language of radical trust is a "both/and" language, a language inclusive of diversity, and I believe it is the language the early Christian writers struggled to find in their attempts to convey the awe-full truth of a God who took on the vulnerability of humanity, of a God crucified by human fear, of a God whose Spirit dwells among and within us.

The gospel of Jesus Christ is a call to risk the practice of radical trust, to risk becoming the interconnected, interdependent body of Christ, and it is a promise that we do not undertake such risk alone. I go to the Eucharist to offer myself to God in thanksgiving, and I go in the context of community. Together, we receive the offering of God, the body and blood of Christ. The offering and receiving are acts of radical trust, of openness to the gifts of the Other. They are the foundation of church as community.

Grounding in Community

As a woman and as one who does theology from a feminist perspective, I am acutely aware that our churches, as institutions, more often manifest the dynamics of fear than those of radical trust.

The hierarchical structure, patriarchal ethos, and often exclusive attitude of the institutional church have combined to marginalize women and all who can be categorized as Other, including the God who seeks communion with us yet refuses to be limited by the capacity of our imaginings. So, what do I do with the recognition that for those who are oppressed, trust may well lead to further oppression? How do I reconcile a feminist "hermeneutic of suspicion" with a call to radical trust? Why do I stay in the church — in my case, the Episcopal church?

First, the practice of radical trust is not the practice of passive acceptance, for it demands that we suspect the power of fear to turn us in upon ourselves and away from community with the Other. Radical trust is conscious of the dynamics of power in our personal and institutional relationships and intentional in its openness to the difficult questions — and often uncomfortable answers — found in the territory of paradox and ambiguity. Such consciousness and intentionality foster resistance to further oppression.

Second, a hermeneutic of suspicion — the imperative to ask how a text, a theology, or a religious institution, is biased to maintain an oppressive status quo — is grounded in the trust that liberating interpretations and actions are possible. Not only do I trust that liberating interpretations and actions are possible, but I also trust that awareness of how our texts, theologies, and institutional structures have served as instruments of oppression will lead ultimately to the struggle for, and commitment to, new visions and new practices.

Finally, the call to radical trust keeps me in the church, although — to use a term Elisabeth Schüssler Fiorenza has taken from Hebrew Scripture to describe the position of the feminist scholar in the academy — I remain something of a "resident alien."[1] Hope and meaning emerge when I pay attention to the concrete particularities of my own parish and seminary communities: to Bill who founded a Saturday night dinner program for persons with HIV/AIDS before dying himself, to Linda's work with coal miners in western Virginia, to Jeff's writing and teaching about the theological dimensions of the ecological issues our human communities must face, to Hannah's commitment to the people of El Salvador, and to the many others who live at the edge, offering themselves in radical trust. We have each been tempted to abandon the institutional church, yet with all its imperfection and ambiguity, we find in the church an essential grounding in community. Those of us of like minds could gather in a new community, but we would only be imitating what we have left behind, practicing the same pattern of exclusion but with a different group of "others."

Like the house Lee and I are building in Vermont, the church is in process, a continuous project that is re-formed by even the smallest act undertaken with care and self-forgetting attention. The challenge is to stay, to dwell in the depths of our connections, connections rooted in paradox, formed in Eucharist, and practiced in radical trust.

Anne Clarke Brown

Chapter 19

SURVIVING THE SECOND GREAT REFORMATION

Virginia Ramey Mollenkott

Virginia Ramey Mollenkott, Ph.D., is professor of English at the William Paterson College in New Jersey and the author of eleven books, including *Sensuous Spirituality: Out from Fundamentalism* (1992), *Women of Faith in Dialogue* (1987), *Godding: Human Responsibility and the Bible* (1987), and *The Divine Feminine: Biblical Imagery of God as Female* (1983). Two of her early books are now classics: *Is the Homosexual My Neighbor? Another Christian View* (with Letha Dawson Scanzoni, 1978, rev. ed. 1994) and *Women, Men, and the Bible* (1977, 1988). She served on the National Council of Churches' committee to prepare *An Inclusive Language Lectionary: Readings for Years A, B, and C,* and was a stylistic consultant for the New International Version of the Bible. Those who hear Virginia at her many public speaking engagements report that her message somehow is always "grace to you, and peace."

On 23 November 1992, emblazoned on the cover of *Time* magazine were these words: "God and Women: A Second Reformation Sweeps Christianity." *Good*, I thought, *the sexual apartheid government of Christianity is receiving notice that the feminist challenge will not go away.* Eventually, either that inequitable mountain is going to move, or millions of women and concerned men *will* move — out of Christianity, joining in an exodus of staggering proportions.

Those of us who are currently alive do not have the luxury of waiting until the dust settles in order to practice our faith. We are forced to decide now concerning how we will survive this major crisis in the life of the church. I understand this book to be a kind of survival handbook. By telling each other our personal survival strategies, we can stimulate greater awareness and confidence in one another. Perhaps we can even come up with some plans for expediting the second Reformation.

When I am guest lecturing somewhere, my favorite moment comes when the formal presentation is over and the floor is opened for questions, comments, and discussion. Similarly, in the college classrooms where I have taught English language and literature for more than forty years, my favorite moments occur when students raise questions and press for clarity about some aspect of the topic at hand. So I am going to indulge myself by structuring this essay in a question-and-answer format. The questions were raised by June Steffensen Hagen, but I have heard similar questions from women (and men) all over the United States. Here, then, are some of my personal survival strategies.

How Did You Get to Where You Are Without Losing Heart?

The fact is that I had no consciousness of mission and therefore of "heart" until my mid-thirties, when feminist authors raised my consciousness and stirred me to transform my life into something liberated and authentic. I had, of course, a conventionally Christian awareness of the indwelling Holy Spirit, but the God I learned at church and home was so distant, fearsome, and controlling that I had no feeling of a supportive Presence in the divine sphere — and very little supportiveness in the human sphere as well.

Yet even before I "came alive," Someone was surely guiding my path. Even with the low self-esteem of an unhealed incest victim (not yet a "survivor"), I had managed to achieve a Ph.D. in literature, which was simultaneously the paper credential that opened many doors and the academic training that made it possible for me to develop a second specialization in feminist theology.

Who was and is that Someone who had been guiding me long before I had any consciousness that life could and should be rich, fulfilling, full of laughter, discovery, and honesty? Is that Someone (that Inner Guide) a supernatural being or rather the deepest and wisest aspect of my own being?

To tell the truth, that is no longer an issue for me. I have come to understand that "our brains mathematically construct objective reality by interpreting frequencies that are ultimately projections from another dimension, a deeper order of existence that is beyond both space and time. The brain is a hologram enfolded in a holographic universe."[1] Such comments from the "new physicists" have improved my comprehension of such Bible passages as Colossians 1:17, which says that all things consist by the Christ. On holographic film, "every small fragment . . . contains all the information recorded in the whole."[2]

So if my Inner Guide is simply my deepest wisdom, that wisdom consists by and enfolds within itself the entire Christ-nature. I am connected not only to the Creator but also to the whole creation, including all of humankind and all natural phenomena (even the stars!) and all spiritual beings (even my loved ones who have left this planet, as well as all the angels and ministers of grace!). I am never alone, never judged, always lovingly supported. With so much happy inner companionship, how could I lose heart?

Not that I haven't needed all the help I could get. Because I come from fundamentalism and still utilize much evangelical methodology, and because my degree is in English rather than religion, my welcome from theological professionals has not been warm. (But at the level of women and men simply looking for clarity and hope, I have been warmly and joyously received.) On the other hand, because I am an open, self-affirming lesbian woman and my social attitudes are liberationist, the religious right has repudiated me. For instance, the president of Bob Jones University (where I earned my bachelor's degree) has written on the university letterhead that I am "a devil" and expressed his opinion that "it would not be unfit to pray for her destruction." So the encouragement of friends (external and internal) has been vital to my survival.

More importantly, social structures change very slowly, and sometimes the struggle to build a more just society feels like the old "one step forward, two steps back" routine. It is for that very reason that we women need to spend some time on the inner processing of our experience as frequently as possible, preferably every day. For me that includes journaling, meditating, reading what inspires me, praying, or just plain sitting, especially in my garden or next to the lake that fronts our home. I need constant contact with the interconnected universe of which I am an aspect, and with the divine energy that is fully present in every aspect of that holographic universe (including, hallelujah, me!). The connection is always there, but I need daily conscious reminders of it.

To say it more simply: In the words of the famous Steven Spielberg movie, every day the Eternal says to each of us, "E.T., call home." Our response determines our happiness.

What Holds You in the Church?

Because of the idolatrously androcentric language of *The Book of Common Prayer*, I am unable to attend church regularly. Nevertheless, I give a weekly contribution to the local congregation of the Episcopal church. As a feminist theologian, I am often present at worship services held at colleges, seminaries, and conferences. I feel that the lesbian and gay Christian community and the feminist Christian community are my real church families. Both, of course, are exceedingly ecumenical.

I believe that the essential church, Christ's Body, is invisible and spiritual, just as the seventeenth-century English poet and theologian John Milton did. Then there is also the visible church, divided not only into individual denominations but also further subdivided in attitudes toward the Bible and various social issues. I think that many feminists feel they have "left the church" when actually they have left only a religious organization, some segment of the visible church. If we have opened ourselves to an authentic awareness of God's presence within us, we *are* the church. And wherever two or three of us are gathered together, the Christ is in the midst of us — at WomanChurch, at Church Women United, at the Evangelical and Ecumenical Women's Caucus, or in some living room somewhere.

Because he was offended by clergy corruption, John Milton did not attend church during all the years he was writing *Paradise Lost, Paradise Regained,* and *Samson Agonistes.*[3] But those magnificent works are ample proof of the depth of his spirituality. He *was* the church, and he knew it.

Or, as Alice Walker puts it in *The Color Purple,* those who come to church hoping to find God will be sadly disappointed. The only way to find God in church is to bring her in with you.[4] The purpose of the visible church is to *share* God.

Sometimes, though, when people ask "What holds you in the church?," they're really asking "Why do you still identify yourself as Christian?" And that also is a good question. I am as disgusted as anybody else with the way the "Christian" majority drags its heels where social justice is concerned, failing to confront the brutal economic policies that cause world hunger and poverty, refusing (still) to grant genuine equal partnership to women, and not only refusing first-class citizenship to openly lesbian women and gay men but even bragging about it. But this is a complex and highly specialized society, and the only way to affect legal policies and social attitudes is through organizations. Religious organizations, even if they do not implement their own idealism, are at least nominally idealistic. They are theoretically the most promising agents of social change — and it is up to feminist and other activists to keep calling church people to accountability to their own stated ideals. The Bible, which is the church's book, insistently calls for righteousness (justice) and therefore is a very effective stimulus to social change. The idea is continually to face the church with liberating interpretations of its own book, asking for implementation of what the organization claims to believe.

But how long can we endure the postponement of justice? That is, I think, a very individual matter. I encourage myself to be patient by reflecting on the fact that wherever a large number of individuals has a vote (such as at ecclesiastical general conventions and assemblies), progress is of necessity very slow. On the issue of ordaining known homosexuals, for instance, the majority in both the Presbyterian and Episcopalian sexuality study groups, having become informed concerning human sexuality, voted that openly homosexual persons should be eligible for ordination. But when the matter went to the floors of the national conventions, those decisions were reversed or further delayed. Why?

Two reasons: Because many uninformed people were voting, and because a lot of right-wing lobbying had gone on behind the scenes. So we must certainly do everything we can to educate people at the grass roots, and we must learn to lobby more effectively.

As for me personally: Why do I still identify with Christianity? For the same reason, in part, that Sartaz Asiz still identifies with Islam, despite the atrocities committed against her country of Bangladesh by Pakistani Muslims. As I explained in my book Sensuous Spirituality, Asiz was horrified that the purity of Islam was used to justify rape and murder. And yet she did not repudiate Islam. Instead, she turned in a radical way to the very roots of Islam, separating from those roots any excrescences of domineering patriarchy. She explains that she could not repudiate Islam because Islam was the context in which she came to understand herself. Instead, she dedicated herself to proving that a person cannot be a good Muslim without struggling against patriarchy, as Muhammad did.[5]

Similarly, I cannot repudiate Christianity because it is the context in which I came to know myself as a social being and a feminist. Furthermore, I know that Jesus drew to himself a society of equals, as Elisabeth Schüssler Fiorenza has documented in her book *In Memory of Her*.[6] So heteropatriarchy is antithetical to the teaching and behavior of Jesus, and I have dedicated myself to proving that one cannot be a good Christian without struggling against heteropatriarchy, as Jesus did.

Furthermore, all effective long-term activism must be nourished by a mythos of one sort or another. As a gardener, I know that no plant will grow if I lop off its roots, and the same is true of an activism that is not undergirded by firm faith. Without faith in a profound symbol system, burnout is inevitable; or worse yet, egotistical limelight-grabbing. Although all religious traditions move me to one degree or another, Christianity is the mythos that carries the deepest resonance for me. Not only have I been in love with Jesus all my life, but I know myself through Christian symbols. I would be foolish to cut myself off at the ankles.

And finally, I remain within Christianity for reasons that are deeply unconscious. How can I know about those reasons if they are unconscious? Through dreams. I have dreamed of Jesus as a lumberjack who saved my life, as a "date" who taught me what nonjudgmental love *feels* like, and as Jane, the mayor of New York City, who fried five eggs and fed a multitude with them.

But perhaps the most telling dream was the one about the cyclone. I was standing near a cathedral when far away I saw a dreadful cyclone dipping and whirling through the sky. I did not know what to do to survive the storm. I asked guidance from a glorious androgynous angel who was standing calmly on the cathedral steps. With her/his eyes, the angel indicated that I should hide under a nearby table. Only as I reconstructed the dream in my waking hours did I realize that I associated the table with the one in Salvador Dali's painting of *The Last Supper*. So I knew that, for me, survival lay in sheltering myself under the table of Jesus the Christ.

And I still know that.

Who or What Calls You to Continue?

I have already explained why I continue to identify with Christianity, so I will interpret this question to mean, "Who calls me to continue my work in the world: teaching, writing, working toward human harmony by overcoming divisiveness, especially sexism and heterosexism?" In this work, human need calls me to continue. My own nature calls me to continue. My Inner Guide calls me to continue. And my communities of accountability call me to continue.

Who are those communities? Most primary of all, the lesbian Christian community and the feminist and womanist Christian communities, the liberationist communities (especially the gay Christian activists), the ecumenical community, and the inter-religious community that seeks understanding among the various faith-traditions. I would hate to let any of them down. But in terms of priorities, if I were forced to go with one community's agenda in conflict with another's, I would take my stand with my lesbian Christian sisters and my womanist/feminist sisters. Although all of creation is spiritually connected, so that all people are "my people" and I in turn belong to everyone, in terms of human limits my heart answers the call particularly of these my sisters.

What Hope Do You Hold Out for Yourself and the Church and the Other Women in It?

I hold out the hope of a new world that's already on its way, a partnership society of peace and mutual sharing, a kindom of God on earth (I like to drop the *g* in "kingdom" in order to achieve a nonclassist, familial term for the realm of God).

How can I believe in that vision in the face of this violent and inequitable society? Well, I can believe because Jesus told me to pray for God's kindom to come, for God's will to be done on earth as it is in heaven — and I trust that Jesus would not have perpetrated a cruel hoax upon us by asking us to pray for the impossible. The Bible contains many prophecies of a righteous society, and I believe they will come true.

I believe in a better future also because the yearning for peace and justice has become so widespread that it is nearing a critical mass. For instance, when I was growing up lesbian in the '30s and '40s, nobody ever said a kind word about homosexuals, and the only references in books and magazines labeled us either sinful or sick. Anybody who spoke about ordaining a homosexual Christian would have been considered lunatic. But here in the '90s, several mainline churches are nearing a critical mass concerning justice for lesbian and gay people, while the United Church of Christ and the Unitarian Universalists have already moved beyond that point. The mountain of heterosexism has begun to move. And that could only happen through the movement of God herself within human history.

Similarly, at a time when the secular women's movement has been declared dead by many "authorities," the church is being forced to recognize that it is up against a second Reformation because the movement of religious women is far from dead. Again, the achievement of critical mass is nearing, and the mountain of sexism is beginning to move.

Several years ago I was speaking at an Episcopal student gathering where the Bible teacher was Bishop Desmond Tutu of South Africa. At that time Nelson Mandela was still in jail and apartheid seemed distressingly unassailable. I asked Bishop Tutu how he maintains joy, and his response was similar to what I have been saying here. Since that time, Desmond Tutu has become an archbishop and Nobel prizewinner, Mandela has been released, and elections have taken place in which all races have voted. Mandela now heads the South African government. The mountain of apartheid has moved! Watching and giving thanks for such developments is a great strengthener of my faith.

Finally, I believe that a better world is on the horizon because of the kind of God who reveals herself to me when I pray and meditate. No, she is not a woman although I use feminine pronouns to offset the androcentrism of the term *God*. But she is not a man, either. She is all-embracing Consciousness, Mind, or Spirit, and she is totally nonjudgmental and loving toward all her children. She is moving us inexorably toward the time when her will is going to be done on earth as it is in heaven.

So we can take heart: We are playing a role in God's drama, and it's a divine comedy. We ourselves may not be on this planet when the play reaches its climax, but we'll be somewhere in the universe or beyond (somewhere in the Christ-nature). And we can trust that the conclusion will be a happy one.

According to 1 Corinthians 15:28, the time will come when God will be "all in all." Since the God who reveals herself to those who will be still, look, and listen, is a nonjudgmental and totally loving Being, we may be sure that when God is "all in all," every creature will be happy and fulfilled. Including us. And that ought to be hope enough for anybody.

What Words Can You Offer Thoughtful Christian Women Who Find the Struggle Continuing — and Exhausting?

My chief word would be this: Don't try to do everything — because you can't. Instead, relax, and ask your Inner Guide to make clear to you what is authentically *your* work and what could just as well be done by somebody else. Preserve yourself, so you can live to see another day.

I find that my energy level rises when I take care to cultivate the attitude of gratitude. No matter how bad things get, there is always something to be thankful for, even if it's only that I'm still breathing. (Breath is a really wonderful gift when you think about it.) The day my mother died, I was so grateful that I was permitted to be with her, holding her, and singing her home, that my predominant emotion was joyfulness.

When someone says something nasty about our motives, beliefs, or strategies, we can be grateful that they aren't God — or, alternatively, that they aren't able to burn us at the stake, as we would no doubt have been burnt in a former era. (We certainly don't condone or rejoice in what was done to our foremothers, but we can be grateful that our nation's political system protects our right to agitate for social change.) A grateful heart is a gateway to longevity and happiness.

Part of self-preservation is making time for fun. For nourishing our relationships with partners, family, and friends. For whatever we most enjoy. And for prayer, meditation, attending the theater, going to art museums, journaling, gardening, inspirational reading — whatever nourishes the awareness that we are not alone . . . that the spiritual resources of the universe are available to help us . . . that God herself watches above us, works through us, and lives within us.

Virginia Ramey Mollenkott

Chapter 20

TAKING THE INCARNATE GOD SERIOUSLY

Elisabeth Moltmann-Wendel

Elisabeth Moltmann-Wendel, Ph.D., lives in Tübingen, Germany, and is a noted theologian and writer, especially in the fields of women, church, and feminist theology. She was born in Herne, Westfalen, grew up in Potsdam, began to study theology in Berlin, and finished with a dissertation at Göttingen. In 1952 she married Jürgen Moltmann, also a theologian, who became professor of theology in Bonn and Tübingen. Together they wrote *Humanity in God* (1993) and *God — His and Hers* (1991). In 1988 she published *A Land Flowing with Milk and Honey*. Her early book *The Women Around Jesus* (1982) united the powers of imagination and theological inquiry in so striking a way that many Christian feminists consider the book crucial to their own spiritual development.

Why am I still in the church?

I am often asked this question in view of our ever-emptier state churches here in Germany where I live, with their bodiless sermons and their lifeless rituals, which particularly fail to contemplate women. And yet, at the ecclesiastical edges — in workshops, in academies for adult training, at church congresses that draw thousands of people — I see so much life growing that could also reach our churches at their center.

When I look at my own story, I find that a process has gone on in my own life that is similar to the development I would wish for others and for the church, a process that has led away from masculine thought categories and lifestyles and toward my own lifestyle and my own visions of a new community of women and men.

Roles

When women first gained a firm foothold in the male church, they attempted to speak this society's language, play its roles, and accept its rhythms. The more they gained self-confidence and became aware of their own thoughts and feelings about life, however, the more they began to feel that this was not their language, that the words hardly reflected their experiences at all.

To illustrate this from my own background, I grew up in Germany in an environment friendly to women. To study theology in that context, after the Second World War, posed absolutely no problems, for me or for my family. My female high school teacher had a doctorate in theology. Our pastor's wife had herself been a pastor and — so it seemed to me — was brighter than her husband. All around me, women were managing pastorates. The legal difficulties that this still posed seemed solvable. At any rate I was more interested in lectern and desk than in pulpit and altar. My theology professors encouraged me. Theology, in particular its existential and political aspects, fascinated me. The discrimination of which many women in this phase of life today complain was unknown to me. Perhaps I was simply not aware of it.

Then I married and thereby lost the right to further training, ordination, and a pastorate. Still I didn't perceive this as a problem. After all, I wanted to have children as well as time for them and for my husband. Even when I asked the lay preacher in our village in Siegerland whether as a woman and a theologian I would be allowed to speak up during his lessons, and he gazed at me intently and finally said: "You may ask questions!" I found it amusing rather than offensive. As a woman, one did not delve too deeply into such things.

What being silenced actually means for women — how it destroys the inner, independent, alive, spontaneous part of their personhood — first dawned on me much later, as the rift between me and my independent past grew wider, as my modes of expression and my desire to argue became weaker, as with the loss of my own name a piece of hard-won identity slipped away.

I began to be influenced by my children's world, by the things they experienced with which I now identified, by my own experiences of motherhood. The experiences with my own body that gave them life. The high times of pregnancy, the adventure of giving birth, the painful and beautiful moment of cutting the umbilical cord, illnesses and exhaustion as a result of it all. The practice, repeated again and again, of letting go. The happiness of achievement — always short-lived and deceptive, should a mother try to rest on her laurels. Life as the giving of oneself.

Something in me rebelled against it all. Against resignation. Against the talk of being satisfied with healthy children, with a nice husband who even helped out with the housework. Against the exhausted silence each evening when women listen to their "working" husbands say their piece. The small freedoms that women allow themselves — an hour at one's desk, the little trip, the rest cure, the beauty farm — did not seem to help much. The question "Who are you?" was increasingly wrenched away, losing its relevance because it could no longer be answered. Silence was a woman's way of life. "Women should remain silent in the churches!" (1 Cor. 14:35). And so she was all the more willing to invest herself elsewhere and in others. Life secondhand.

Revolution

It sounds banal and theologically hackneyed to say what I began to grasp in the early '70s, upon reading articles by American feminists that friends passed on to me: You are God's creation, all of you, with all your sense and abilities, with all your interest in intellectual matters, with your rational abilities and with those of which you are unaware, of which you don't want to take notice. You are a woman in a situation that does not satisfy you. You are not just a partner. You are you. You are whole. There is nothing wrong with you.

In that summer of 1972 the world seemed to make a 180-degree turnaround. I realized that something totally new was beginning that would not only radically change my opinions but also my values. A cultural revolution. The things according to which I had oriented myself, which were valued as civic virtues — performance, making one's way, forging intellectual inroads, self-control, women's self-limitation, controlling one's emotions, the body, and nature — these were not eternal, lofty values. They were not God's beloved creation. They were the products of a male culture and highly questionable because as a consequence of them, minorities — people of color, Jews, and especially women — were oppressed. Through these values, nature was exploited; they were imposed upon the earth by force. These values made living things mute, mutilated, dead. And, most disturbingly, these values were cultivated by Christianity, proclaimed from the pulpit, practiced in the churches: Subdue the earth, deaden your bodies and their desires, humble yourselves before God's almighty hand. And women, the most faithful churchgoers of all, had particularly internalized all of this. We were an ever-prepared host of servants, programmed for self-surrender by the constant activation of guilt feelings. These values foster a theology in which self-love could never develop, which on the basis of its one-sided male worldview perceived self-realization only as elbowing one's way ahead and therefore forbade it for women while applauding it for men.

When I began to make my thoughts public, I encountered a surprisingly positive response. We women set off on our way, learning to love each other, to feel, to search. It was not always easy. Pearl S. Buck tells in one of her stories of how a young Chinese woman had her feet unbound in order to be freed from the unworthy, mincing walk that prevented her from going her own way, and how many torments and tears this liberation cost her. It was impossible for her to rid herself of the handicap completely, but she was certainly able to learn to walk more freely and independently. It wasn't always easy to rewind the film of life. For many it was impossible to build an independent existence once again. It was and remains difficult not to live up to what is expected of a Christian woman. One may exercise previously unexerted ego-strength to be able to say "no" and to appear hard-hearted. It is a curious feeling to revive the body one had spurned long ago and to "be" a body once again, to "understand" with the body.

At a conference during that time, a woman came up to me and tried to impress upon me that we should do feminist theology. She gave me a long paper with a theory about deductive and inductive theology, according to which feminist theology was inductive because it grew out of experience and was able to express the concerns of those who had long been mute. For me, it was too theoretical. I was still trying to figure out my new existence, to understand with my body, to find my own form of expression. What had accompanied me along my long theological road and had given me freedom and spontaneity continued to be valid for me: the knowledge — which I had discovered in the young Luther — that we have been liberated to spontaneity in God's unconditional acceptance; the Eastern Orthodox image of a God flowing all around us, forgetting our guilt rather than judging us; the Protestant hymn-poet Paul Gerhardt's liberating, sensual mysticism:

> *O das mein Sinn ein Abgrund wär*
> *und meine Seel ein weites Meer,*
> *das ich dich möchte fassen.*

> *Oh, were my mind an abyss*
> *my soul the widest sea,*
> *that I might fathom thee.*[1]

American tours de force such as that of feminist Mary Daly —
who considers the whole of theology patriarchal, inimical to women,
and enamored of death — seem to me to be tarnished by a want of
factual knowledge. God the Father was never a nightmare to me. The
great Mother, whom many women have discovered as the ground
of all being, seems to me, in view of our own lack of images and
history, an interesting figure with which to identify. But beyond that,
she seems to contribute more to the regression than to the transformation of society. A new religiosity with absolute claims and covert
intolerance, complete with new moral prerogatives and categories,
seems to me to be the greatest enemy to date of our newly realized
approach to finding ourselves. We, who are all so different, are, for
fear of being left alone, in danger of submitting ourselves to new
rules of sisterhood, thus suppressing the development of the process
toward real sisterhood, obstructing the art of being different.

Research

Two things have become important to me: first, to expose the
insidious processes that lead to the patriarchalization of the gospel,
of which women were either not aware or which they allowed to
occur; and second, to ask: Where do women today get their strength
to live? The first question belongs to the realm of historical theology
and the second to practical theology. To try to answer them means
for me to do feminist theology. From the perspective of a woman
affected by these matters, I want to investigate our history and to
ferret out possibilities for our life together.

Despite all the niches that I have discovered for myself in
theology, it has become increasingly evident to me to what extent
our written, fixed Christian documents have been shaped by men.
They reflect a male perception of the self and of the world. There are
statements that affect women directly, humiliate them, or make them
ridiculous, to be found everywhere from the Bible to Karl Barth, and
beyond. Thus one reads in Sirach 25:24: "From a woman sin had its
beginning, and because of her we all die." Or Thomas Aquinas says
that the woman is a stunted man and not created in the image of
God. Beyond this, there is also a hidden sexism, an unspoken op-

pression of the female sex, as when for example an entire segment of our cultural heritage such as the hymnal silently assumes the man to be the actual Christian person. Thus we sing in church, "may God care for wife and child" or "good Christian men rejoice." When we are not allowed to name ourselves, we become mute and nameless.

As a result of my own research and that of other women, it has become increasingly clear to me that this was not the case in the early years of Christianity. The first person to proclaim Christianity's central message — the resurrection of Jesus — was a woman, and all the cutting away at this fundamental fact has not been enough to suppress it. Women disciples stood as close to Jesus as his twelve male disciples, remained by him in his death, and were involved in the work of salvation. Yet female names were changed even in the Bible, facts such as the leadership functions of women in the early church were obscured, documents of early and later church history that reflected the leading role of women were destroyed.

It is painful to be reminded again and again not only that a part of women's history was erased, but that the very image of God was also tampered with to accommodate a projection of male wishes and ideas. Jesus' *Abba* (an intimate word reflecting tender disrespect) — the God of the Sermon on the Mount, who causes the sun to rise on the evil and the good, and sends rain on the righteous and unrighteous — became God the Father of Western civilization, who requires order and subordination, who no longer contains us tenderly and sovereignly in the wholeness of nature and spirit. I often feel angry and impotent when I see how the God who loves us unconditionally and liberates us has been transformed into a petty-minded soul who judges us, remonstrates with us, and requires fearful vassals.

Not all women will manage to rediscover this all-encompassing God as a vital force in their lives. Too many humiliating, mortal wounds have been inflicted upon them by theology and the church. Yet others have begun this pilgrimage, have discovered this God in the Bible, in themselves, in their imagination, and in their dreams, and have begun to find a new language. They have broken out of the silence that was imposed on them in God's name. To silence them once again would mean more than squelching a social group. It would mean repressing the liberating experiences of a tradition that belongs at the center of the Christian gospel, that revives the forgotten dimension of wholeness in the lives of all men and women.

Rediscovery

We must now move on to solve our contemporary theological, church-related problems. For me this means rediscovering our jeopardized, forgotten, holy human bodies. It means taking God's incarnation seriously. We can start by considering women's bodies, which are a prime example of male-centered contempt and defamation. We can then continue with the rediscovery of the different bodies that belong to children, men, racial minorities, sick people, all of which have their own rhythms and are an expression of God's incarnation. They are all political organs reflecting both processes of healing and processes of destruction. All bodies challenge us to believe and to act, not only with our head and our will, but also with all of our senses. In order to do this, we need churches that not only have the cross at their center but also have new symbols of wholeness and healing. And we need a language that not only promises reconciliation and communion with God by means of legal concepts but that is also capable of seizing and transforming our existence in its entire physicality. There are already initial efforts in this direction; there are signs of hope. Becoming involved in this process is worth it.

Elisabeth Moltmann-Wendel

Chapter 21

LEAD US NOT INTO TEMPTATION

Mary E. Hunt

Mary E. Hunt, Ph.D., is co-founder and co-director of the Women's Alliance for Theology, Ethics and Ritual (WATER) in Silver Spring, Maryland. She is a Roman Catholic in the women-church tradition who lectures and writes on theology and ethics with particular attention to liberation issues. She spent several years teaching and working on women's issues and human rights in Argentina as a Frontier Intern. Mary is the author of *Fierce Tenderness: A Feminist Theology of Friendship* (1991), an award-winning book. She has contributed to a number of books as well as the *Journal of Feminist Studies in Religion, America, Concilium, Conscience, The Witness,* and others. When Mary Hunt preaches, people listen.

The Temptation: Access to Power

*T*he Names Project quilt exhibited in Washington, D.C., in October 1992, in all of its poignant splendor drew together thousands of people from all over the country. On the closing afternoon of what had been an emotionally taxing weekend, I preached at the Interfaith Healing Service for People with AIDS at the National Cathedral. The service was splendid with choirs and soloists, banners and candles, thousands of worshipers and religious leaders from many denominations. I had not thought too much about it in advance but simply prepared my sermon as I do when I am invited as a Roman Catholic feminist theologian to preach at local Protestant churches.

I arrived at the enormous church and found my place in the procession with other clergy and lay leaders, discovering that I was to process just in front of the rector. Since my partner's parents were coming for the weekend, I had been more preoccupied with staining the deck of our home than with ecclesial details. Suddenly I realized that my part in the service was far more central than I had thought. As I sat in the nave between the rector and a prominent local pastor, with a rabbi and several political figures, I could not help but think, "What is a good post-Catholic girl like me doing here?"

When it came time to preach, I was escorted up to the pulpit ceremoniously by a verger. As I looked out and down to the congregation, I was struck simultaneously by the fact that one could get a nosebleed at such a height if one were so prone and that looking down at people to preach was in ludicrous contradiction to my message. Nonetheless, I carried out my professional role with aplomb, suggesting in my sermon that when justice is lacking, as it surely is in the case of AIDS, that we double up on love.

Mine was a popular message, a simple idea with a political flair, seemingly just what was needed in the moment. I am convinced that it worked less because of my skill than because of those once-in-a-while graced insights that remind me that something more is going on than I realize.

Preaching the sermon was a professionally fulfilling task, indeed a privilege. More so, it was edifying to see a church used for ecumenical worship during the century's worst pandemic. We were a common people there despite our many backgrounds and beliefs, and we did well what a community does when it is faced with its own finitude. I provided helpful leadership, marshaling years of education, training, and ministry, that because I am an out lesbian, pro-choice Catholic woman, will probably never be used in the church of my baptism.

I left the cathedral ambivalent. I was angry, on the one hand, that my ministry is not acceptable in my own denomination but that I was ironically "the Catholic" on the program in an ecumenical service. On the other hand, perhaps more of necessity than conviction but I will never know, I was relieved that I could go home unshackled to any denomination, indeed that I can read *The New York Times* and drink coffee in the privacy of my home on Sunday mornings and not be wedded to any regular ministerial commitment. This is not because of innate laziness but because of a well-nourished critical capacity to see the problems as well as the temptations in patriarchal religion. After all, feminist, womanist, mujerista, and other women theologians have been pointing these out for decades now all over the world. What has been less apparent is how we are to live religiously beyond these problems and still stay attuned to and be helpful for other people who do not see matters as we do, or at least do not see them as rapidly. The question is pragmatic because at base the issue is integrity.

It was tempting to think about a quick switch to the Episcopal church where I could be ordained priest. Then I began to fantasize the fast track to the episcopacy and a future of liturgical, educational, and theo-political leadership in a denomination that might appreciate my skills. But as I boarded the subway for the mundane ride home, I was snapped back into reality, breathing a little hard thinking about how easy it is for any of us to be lured by misplaced power even when we are in little danger of having access to it.

The Success Problem: Victims of a Little Change

I see the late-twentieth-century problem for feminist women in religion not so much being rejected as being co-opted, not so much being left aside as being worked to death (physically and spiritually) by religious systems that are finally set up to keep unequal power equations humming. The difficulty is that while this is perfectly obvious from the outside, the temptation to change it from within is compelling to those who are acceptable (as I was ever so briefly in the National Cathedral) since the raw human needs for which the ministry is a response are overwhelming. One can feel she is doing something rather than nothing, offering bread not stones although the bread may be staler than it looks on the outside.

The dilemma is what I call a success problem. It is the fruit of so many women's efforts to change patriarchal religions that now that the religions have changed a little we have to rethink our approaches lest we become victims of our own successes. From the suffrage leaders of the late nineteenth century to the ordained women of the present day, myriad strategies have loosened the stranglehold of patriarchy but left some new problems for which my colleagues and I must imagine new solutions.

Catholic women seem to be the most oppressed because ordination, now a given and growing phenomenon in most Protestant denominations, is still elusive. But because of the recalcitrance of the institutional Roman Catholic church, we have been in the vanguard of the women-church movement, an international, ecumenical network of feminist base communities, brought together in sacrament and solidarity. That is where I find my own spiritual sustenance, usually in a small house-church in the Washington, D.C., area, Sisters Against Sexism (SAS), and sometimes on the road with similar groups when I am invited to join them.

In one week, both the U.S. Catholic bishops' decision to give up trying to write a pastoral letter on women and the Church of England's vote at last to ordain women signaled the rapidly accumulating muscle that feminists have in the face of reactionaries. After nine years of trying to write a letter *about* women but not in cooperation *with* them, Catholic clergymen simply had not gotten the message that women and men are equal in creation and therefore equal in terms of ministry. They had not even understood that to write about partnership and not include women among the authors is to miss the fundamental point. That they defeated their own draft of a letter when it came up for a vote is a good example of the fact that new problems emerge for which old solutions are inadequate. The bishops had lots of help from Catholic feminists, not all of which they considered helpful. But these problems push our willingness to stay with the struggle and test our resolve to make all things new when such newness can be exhausting. A closer look at several other issues will make this clear.

First, many of us who have struggled for equal rites/rights are now uninterested in Christianity. It is not simply that we have rejected it wholesale, though the behavior of many church officials would warrant that. Rather, it is that we are bored by it, bored by the antics of ecclesiastical officials to bar the doors and protect the so-called stained glass ceiling. Moreover, I — and I suspect many other honest colleagues — are somewhat bored by the whole religious story of Christianity, the endless repetition of scriptural dicta never followed and the hollow ring of ideals turned platitudes. While I would be the first to credit Christianity, especially Catholicism, with a certain cultural aesthetic and a decided ethical program for living in right relation, I find it in the breech rather than as the norm.

I see equally valiant efforts, often with better results, elsewhere. Religious traditions like Buddhism, Wicca, Judaism, etc., have a great deal to offer those of us who grew up as Christians. Learning about them and even practicing those aspects that "fit" are not exercises in reckless eclecticism but part of a lifelong religious search. I now see efforts to keep us inside the picket fences of our own traditions as a way to prevent the cross-fertilization that feminists have learned is so vital to our growth in things spiritual. Who says that we can't celebrate the Winter Solstice and the Festival of Lights, bless houses and horses, and drink from a common cup?

Some critics try to psychologize away my claim to a certain boredom with Christianity as the product of being hurt, excluded, demeaned by the Christian community. Of course all of that is true, but there is a difference between boredom and righteous anger even though a creative solution to both is moving in new directions without getting stuck in endlessly unproductive conversation. In other religious traditions I find new material for pondering the questions of meaning and value, for designing ways to live well personally and as part of the common good, and I want to pay attention to it. I know the grass is always greener, and that all religious traditions have their problems. But comparative religious input is spiritually helpful. It is the blinders on most mainline Christian denominations that would confine even my protests to Christianity. That is boring.

Second, indebted to the insightful work of feminist law professor Catherine MacKinnon, whose notion that gender is constructed to perpetuate dominance not to explain difference, is convincing to me; I am both intrigued and unmoved by goddesses. Why not think of the divine in feminine terms to balance the centuries of masculinist religion? Of course, but by the same token if it is dominance and not difference we are dealing with, why further reinforce the stereotypes and hence exacerbate the dominance by insisting on "gendering" the concept of the divine? I do not have an answer, but the question is now part of my spiritual concerns, not something even the most progressive churches have even imagined as they continue to wrangle over inclusive language, a tiny nugget of the same, much bigger matter.

Another late-twentieth-century problem that highlights just how pernicious religion can be as a social force is the remarkable segregation of virtually all religious groups. Even the women-church movement, predicated on the notion that women must be church in order to survive, indeed that our being church will change churches, remains very Euro-American. While there are women from a range of different cultural groups who are part of the movement, it is not clear that the term "women-church" is either as congenial or helpful in naming their reality as it has been in naming mine.

What this means to me is that those of us who have found something of a home in women-church must choose between perpetuating racism or following pioneer feminist theologian Nelle Morton's insight that "the journey is home."[1] In this case, it means forsaking any ultimacy we may have mistakenly placed in women-church for a much broader call to religious agency — that is, the right and responsibility of adults to make their own decisions when it comes to religion — a right all women have regardless of the name and/or occupation they choose. I urge this shift for those who might reify women-church in a way that will finally be as limiting to human community as many other churches have been. And I insist on it after seeing just how damaging this racism can be to even the most well-intentioned attempts at being community in a society that is structured to keep power in the hands of white people.

The Isolation: Ordination as a Gatekeeper

This call to religious agency is answered by some women as a call to ordained ministry. That is the option I toyed with in the Cathedral, since changing denominations would at least bring me closer to ordination even if other aspects of my biography, especially living proudly as a lesbian, would be practical if not theo-political impediments in all but the Metropolitan Community Church. Having done all of the degree and training requirements, I think about it, especially when I meet people who respond so vibrantly to what I can do as a theologian, ethicist, and sometimes a minister. It is also tempting because denominations offer jobs and paychecks, pension plans and platforms from which to make a difference — all enticing as one matures.

I am forced, however, beyond all of the theo-political issues, to look at ordination per se since clericalism in my religious tradition has been one of the single most serious barriers to spiritual equality. I wonder whether setting some people aside for religious leadership is in itself part of the patriarchal nature of Christianity, something that we perpetuate at our peril even with women in the roles.

Judging from the wonderful women ministers I have come to know through WATER, the Women's Alliance for Theology, Ethics and Ritual, where a group meets monthly for breakfast, education, and support, I can offer counterevidence. But in fact, despite their excellent intentions and creative work, I sense that there is something slightly suspicious about the aura of ordination versus the way in which other professionals go about their work. While it is true that doctors and lawyers take exams and are admitted to their various practices by common consent of their colleagues, and that ordination is yet another form of such gatekeeping alleged to keep up quality, I wonder if the mystique surrounding it and the legal implications it carries de facto (permission by the state to perform marriages, for example) don't deserve to be rethought. Certainly checks and balances regarding continuing education, malpractice, peer review, and sexual abuse need to be structured in if ordination is to be handled responsibly, something that now seems woefully lacking.

This is not an attempt to hijack the profession now that women are finally entering it in unprecedented numbers. Some mainline seminaries report more than fifty percent of their entering students are women. In virtually every Christian denomination that ordains women, the rapid growth in the number of women ministers has surprised even the women. I offer an invitation to try something else, to do the whole thing better now that women are increasingly a part of what is, after all, a recipe for a woman's job in patriarchy: relatively low pay, marginal prestige, long hours, required to nurture. Frankly, that is not the kind of job I want anyone to have. Besides, community care is an essential task in any civilized society, as important as politics, medicine, or law. Hence, an overhaul of the whole notion of ordained leadership, even if the Pope were to invite me personally, will have to precede my acceptance or enthusiastic endorsement of it for anyone, male or female.

The Search: The Root of Spiritual Integrity

I ask myself the question "Then what?" when I realize that even solutions to old problems, much less articulation of new problems, are lacking. For example, even when Catholic women get ordained, I am still left with the fact that Christianity is based on a violent story that women then re-enact in the Eucharist. Is this, all puns intended, overkill?

By the same token, WATER's phone rings with partners asking for liturgical help in shaping memorial services for their lovers who have died of breast or ovarian cancer, women who, like me, find little in the local church to sustain them on a good day, much less to help them deal with, even sort out, things on a bad one. I am grateful that we can offer resources to help meet their needs. But I am left scratching my head about how we will educate the next generation of theologians and ministers to be able to do the work since the only options for training available now carry a content many of my generation have had to unlearn to be effective.

Just to thicken the theological soup, I note that maybe temptation itself is a good thing, maybe the notion of avoiding it is a construct designed to keep women from having the opportunity to make a real difference. Construction is always more difficult than deconstruction, and there is no moral obligation to replace one meaning system with another. But it is perhaps a sign of the times that the search goes on even while I put my best skills to work with people with AIDS, women with breast cancer, crack-exposed "boarder babies," and others who, like myself, see the problems in Christianity faster than we can mold and manage the solutions.

I do not have definitive answers to all of these questions. But the search for answers, at least to trace the contours of some basic sense of what it means to be human in a cosmic context, is the root of my spiritual integrity. It is the same integrity that keeps me out of churches for the most part, yet still longing for ways to be religious that are politically consistent and personally satisfying. I feel well accompanied by many other women, and men, whose search takes similar shape.

Mary E. Hunt

Chapter 22

SPIRIT OF GOD, YOU CAN MAKE US LIVE!

Toinette M. Eugene

Toinette M. Eugene, Ph.D., is associate professor of Christian social ethics at Garrett-Evangelical Theological Seminary in Evanston, Illinois. Her academic expertise and interests center on the African American family and its cultural and religious development, and on feminist and womanist issues. She is the author of *Lifting as We Climb: A Womanist Ethic of Care* (1995) and co-author with James N. Poling of *Balm in Gilead: Pastoral Care for African American Families Experiencing Abuse* (1996, forthcoming). A photographer and potter, she has recently learned the art of African American quilting as a way of reclaiming and rejoicing in her womanist roots and relationships.

*F*rom the prophetic visions of Ezekiel, the Divine Questioner speaks: "My agent, Ezekiel, can these bones live? My agent, Ezekiel, can these bones live?" When it comes to the scatteredness, to the marginalization, to the fragmentation, and to the disintegration of the views of the Christian community on the appropriateness of ministry with and for women and other oppressed groups, the Divine Questioner thunders, "Can these bones live?" When we talk about the ministries already exercised by women and by other alienated or exiled groups in the church and in society, the Divine Questioner persists: "I wonder — I wonder, can these bones live?"

In particular, the subject of women in ministry in Christian churches has long been an issue of controversy. Indeed, there have been times when the debate has become so heated that in its name the relationships of Christians, congregations, and even denominations have been fractured. It may be that even in the present hour God is resolving the debate and setting aside the controversy, for it is an incontestable fact that an ever-increasing number of women are preaching and teaching the gospel, answering yes to the all-compelling call of God.

The Divine Questioner asks with haunting urgency in these days ending oppressive apartheid in South Africa, "My agent, Ezekiel, can these bones live?" Mercy Oduyoye, a Ghanian, and deputy general secretary of the World Council of Churches, has already forthrightly acted out her answer: "Thou knowest, O Lord!" The Divine Questioner asks with unrelenting necessity in the Philippines to a daily communicant, former President Corazon Aquino, "Can these bones live?" "Thou knowest, O Lord!" And without ceasing, the question is put to the mothers of the Plaza de Mayo, who demonstrate in the names of the members of their families who have been unjustly abducted in Argentina and elsewhere in Latin America. Rigoberta Menchu has offered her Nobel Peace Prize as a clue to what is possible in reply. "Thou knowest, O Lord!" The first African American woman United States Senator, Carol Moseley-Braun, has come forth to signal her affirmation in these trying times for her sisters, for her people, and for all underrepresented constituencies.

The question is posed to those women whose children and whose husbands and lovers have disappeared, presumably reduced to a pile of dry and dead bones: "Oh, Ezekiel, can these bones live?" The question is reiterated by welfare mothers, unwed mothers, and widowed women who live not far from many beautiful cathedral doors, "Wait a minute, Ezekiel, what about the odds? Can these bones live?"

In the prophetic passage in Ezekiel 37, the Divine Being called upon Ezekiel to proclaim to the exiles in Babylon words not only of lamentation, mourning, and woe but also appointed him to speak words of reconciliation and resurrection. To a chosen messenger who was so gentle that during the Babylonian captivity, he sat where the people sat and not among the more distinguished folk, God demanded that he get up and preach a revival sermon to a bunch of dry bones. God demanded that Ezekiel persist in his unwelcome task, whether the people heard or refused to hear, so that "they will know that there had been a prophet among them" (Ezek. 2:5, author's translation).

Ezekiel was a sign that God was not through with what had begun with the surrender of Jerusalem to Babylon, nor was God through with the exiles. To know and to understand what God did mean, the people needed a prophetic and a priestly minister who was capable of passing on the Good News that the Spirit of God would bring them to life again. Ezekiel's priestly and prophetic task was to call the people to a new form of liberating and liberated existence in which all activity and generativity would be modeled upon the nondiscriminating and all-inclusive life of God. God promised, "I will put my spirit within you, and you shall live" (Ezek. 37:14). And when God makes promises, she does not take them back. And so Ezekiel was inspired and compelled to speak the words of the prophecy. A prophetic utterance appears in the chapter that precedes chapter 37 and repeats with expanded emphasis the promise of God uttered through the one God chose:

> *The nations shall know that I am the Sovereign One, says God,*
> *when in their sight I prove my holiness through you. For I will*
> *take you away from among the nations and gather you from all*

*the foreign lands, and bring you back to your own land. For I
will sprinkle clean water upon you to cleanse you from all your
impurities. . . . I will give you a new heart and place a new spirit
within you, taking from your bodies your stony hearts and
giving you natural hearts. I will put my spirit within you . . . .
you shall be my people and I will be your God.* (Ezek. 36:23-28,
author's translation)

I Will Put My Spirit Within You, and You Shall Live.

These passages clearly state that the Spirit is given to *all* persons, women as well as men, without discrimination, and the promise is made manifest — these bones can live!

Such texts suggest that we might have some strong support in
saying that women have always been intended in pastoral and
indeed priestly ministry, patriarchal bias to the contrary. The Christian church was launched on a prophetic platform of nondiscrimi-
nation against women. When the Holy Spirit came at Pentecost,
Peter's sermon, quoting Joel, declared what had already been said
in Ezekiel:

*And it shall come to pass in the last days, says God, I will
pour out my spirit on all flesh: and your sons and your
DAUGHTERS shall prophecy. . . . Yes, even on my servants
and HANDMAIDS I will pour out a portion of my spirit . . . and
they shall prophesy.* (Acts 2:17-18, author's translation)

The text was good enough for Peter, who was a very conservative preacher, to say the least. Peter was first under obligation to
explain that the strange behavior manifested in the upper room was
spiritual ecstasy and not intoxication. Then he proceeded to reach
back, quoting the prophet Joel, to say that this was, in fact, what God
had promised would happen. Now at Pentecost God was doing it:
pouring out the Spirit on *all* flesh, on Mary and on the Magdalene,
even on the disciples who had disowned their Master — God was
doing it anyway — pouring out the Spirit on all flesh. The revelation was not admonishing male exclusivism, per se, but it was

declaring the generous outpouring of the Holy Spirit, after which both sons and *daughters* would prophesy.

The foundational proclamation from the text is that God pours out God's Spirit indiscriminantly on all persons to enable priestly and prophetic ministry. Those persons, thereafter, were and are commissioned to bear the message as Jesus proclaimed in Acts 1:8: "You will receive power when the Holy Spirit comes down on you; then you are to be my witnesses in Jerusalem, throughout Judea and Samaria, yes even to the ends of the earth" (author's translation).

This all-inclusiveness — found in Ezekiel, in Joel, in Jeremiah, and repeated in Acts — has long been popular and valid in many liberation-oriented denominations and cultures. God has, for sure, been known by African American women especially to be no respecter of persons, classes, or races. Therefore, as an African American womanist, I rejoice in knowing that in whatever discriminatory areas where we may have experienced suffering, God ultimately intends to deal with all of us and commission all of us without distinction. It remains only for others who have also enjoyed this powerful biblical acceptance and sending forth, or who have on occasion made good use of God's promises to suit our other needs, to also apply this all-embracing acceptance from God to the experience of including women in the outpouring of this lavish ministerial commissioning of God.

The story of God's agent Ezekiel, who found himself preaching to a valley of dry bones, is instructive in our struggle and in formulating our own response to the Divine Questioner: "Oh, Ezekiel, can these bones live?" God tells Ezekiel in no uncertain terms that he is to believe and to proclaim that these dead and dried up remnants of humanity can be brought back to life and be reformed by the Spirit of God. Period. No kidding. "Dem bones gonna rise again!" Not surprisingly, we find that Ezekiel was not a welcome presence to the distributors of religious and secular power in his day. His message — not his maleness — escorted him out to the farthest social fringe of theological respectability. Who wants to hear, "Thus saith the Lord: Get your house in order"?

But Ezekiel continued year after year, in fact for forty-eight chapters of his biblical book, to proclaim the judgment of God upon

Israel and upon Jerusalem, the Holy City. The only impression that he gained from his efforts was that year by year, his audience was becoming more obdurate and obstinate. The crimes against justice and against the weak and oppressed were many — but like today, those who heard him did not hear him, for they persisted in their ways.

They whined and weaseled, like some folk we may know: "Ezekiel, don't push these issues on me: renunciation of my self-aggrandizing way of life, letting go of my unchallenged hold on power. After all, you are a minority voice. Who's complaining that patriarchy is another form of idolatry? Who's suggesting that we are withholding from some people what is theirs by birth, or by vocation, or by dispensation from God? Ezekiel, you accuse us of failing to make the weak sheep strong. Don't you know something about sociology, Ezekiel? Social structures are like pyramids — there isn't enough room at the top for all of us."

A former theology professor of mine encapsulated this resistance most poignantly when he said, "I don't intend to give up my tenure, my position, my security to accommodate any women, much less any minorities into my rank."

"My sense of justice must be tempered by common sense," was his calculated and considered response.

But Ezekiel continued to report his heavenly mandate. He proclaimed, "God is weary — worn out — working me overtime to get you to hear that now is the time to get your house in order. Parity, equity, equal access, legitimate opportunities, just relations are the order of the day!" And Israel resisted and persisted in its self-defined ways to retard the changing and evolving presence of God in the world, like so many of us do today. We keep God in traction — never once realizing that if we profess that God has liberated us from something, then that same God has the right to bring down the barriers that oppress someone else.

But there is a price to be paid for resistance and persistence. Israel and Jerusalem paid its price. The nation, its land, its people suffered through a coup by a pagan power. Judgment seemingly always comes to the people of God first. At least that is the biblical perspective. But with every biblical prophet, the words of doom are almost always followed by a word of hope and comfort, especially to those who are oppressed, repressed, or depressed in seemingly hopeless situations.

God speaks to Ezekiel in the vision of the Valley of the Dry Bones, a metaphor for the House of Israel at the hands of the Babylonians. The chosen people of God are lifeless: limbless, disfigured, disintegrated, divested of wholeness and purpose. God booms out the question to the prophet, with all eternity waiting for an answer. *"Ezekiel, can these bones live?"*

When I look at the reality of struggle, of pain, and of unmerited suffering in the lives of countless women, of countless poor and oppressed people in this world, I tremble with the implications of this question. Can stubborn, self-pitying Israel ever come to life again? Can we, who are so often turned in on ourselves, so set in our ways, so backward looking, can we come alive? What about the burnt-out people, the disregarded, the disenfranchised, the refuse who have been refused by the righteously religious elements of our society? Can these bones live? When I dare to examine the dry bones of some parishes and some people in authority that I have known, and when at last I am forced to examine my own arid and barren soul, the question of God remains, "Can these bones live?" It may be comforting for us to know that this passage of Scripture itself does have a humorous, paradoxical quality about it also, especially when we wait for the prophet to stop squirming and answer God's question, "Can these bones live?"

Ezekiel's response, "God, you alone know that answer," must go down in religious literature as one of the most tactful and diplomatic replies in history to an obviously loaded question: "Can these bones live?" Like many of us, Ezekiel didn't have the nerve to say, "No," but he didn't have the faith to say, "Yes," either. "God, thou knowest," was all he could muster. But unlike Ezekiel, today I won't be quite as evasive in my response. I say for women, for the weak, even for the wrong-headed, as well as for the discouraged and despairing in our midst — for all of us who truly want the Spirit to revive us again: "God, you can make us live."

I say to God for all of us,
Just as soon as your revolution
    has come to our attention,
        you can make us live.
When we have learned to de-genderize
    our understanding of your nature,
        you can make us live.
When we all have felt the pain
    of the powerless,
        you can make us live.
After we have taken our own responsibility
    to protest what is unjust,
        you can make us live.

As we participate totally in the mystery of the Passion,
    the death, and resurrection of the One we call
        the Lily of the Valley, the Rose of Sharon,
            the Bright Morning Star, your Child, Jesus,
we will come to life
    in these dark and dangerous times!
        God, you can make us live!

———————————

Toinette M. Eugene

Notes

Epigraph Page
1. Psalm 68:11, *The Book of Common Prayer* (New York: Oxford University Press, 1979), 677.

Section One, "Writers," Epigraph
1. Sirach 51:22, "A Song of Pilgrimage," *Supplemental Liturgical Texts: Prayer Book Studies* 30 (New York: Church Hymnal Corporation, 1989), 28.

Chapter 1, "Bones," Madeleine L'Engle
1. Madeleine L'Engle, *The Irrational Season* (New York: Seabury Press, 1979), 27.

Chapter 2, "Prospecting," Shirley Nelson
1. Shirley Nelson, *Fair, Clear and Terrible: The Story of Shiloh, Maine* (Latham, NY: British American Publishing, 1989).
2. Elisabeth Schüssler Fiorenza, *In Memory of Her: A Feminist Theological Reconstruction of Christian Origins* (New York: Crossroad, 1983), 33.
3. Elizabeth O'Connor, *Letters to Scattered Pilgrims* (New York: Harper, 1979, 65.
4. Reinhold Niebuhr, "The Christian Witness in the Social and National Order." Address before the first world assembly of the World Council of Churches (Amsterdam, 1948).

Chapter 3, "The Communion of Saints and Sinners,"
Nancy A. Hardesty
1. Charles Williams, *Descent of the Dove* (Grand Rapids, MI: Wm. B. Eerdmans Publishing Company, 1939), and *Descent into Hell* (Grand Rapids, MI: Wm. B. Eerdmans Publishing Company, 1939, 1949).

Chapter 6, "The Wind Shifts," S. Sue Horner
1. Letha Dawson Scanzoni and Nancy A. Hardesty, *All We're Meant to Be: A Biblical Approach to Women's Liberation* (Waco, TX: Word Books, 1974; 3d ed., Grand Rapids, MI: Wm. B. Eerdmans Publishing Company, 1992).
2. Now called the Evangelical and Ecumenical Women's Caucus, its mailing address is Post Office Box 9989, Oakland, CA 94613-0989.

Chapter 7, "Homecoming," Joyce Quiring Erickson
1. Mary Daly, *Beyond God the Father* (Boston: Beacon Press, 1973).

Chapter 8, "Under the Mantle of Mercy," Janet Ruffing
1. Elizabeth Janeway, *The Powers of the Weak* (New York: Knopf, 1980).
2. I especially enjoy the songs of Colleen Fulmer on her albums *Cry of Ramah* (1985) and *Her Wings Unfurled* (1989). They are available through the Loretto Spirituality Network, 725 Calhoun Street, Albany, CA 94709. I also enjoy the work of Miriam Therese Winter, who has recorded numerous albums. See also her book *Woman Prayer/Woman Song: Resources for Ritual* (Oak Park, IL: Meyer Stone, 1987).
3. Caroline Bynum, *Holy Feast and Holy Fast: The Religious Significance of Food to Medieval Women* (Berkeley and Los Angeles: University of California Press, 1987), and *Jesus as Mother: Studies in the Spirituality of the High Middle Ages* (Berkeley and Los Angeles: University of California Press, 1982).
4. Elizabeth Johnson, "Mary, the Female Face of God," *Theological Studies* 50 (1989): 500-526.

Chapter 9, "The Rhythm of Renewal," Marjory Zoet Bankson
1. Nelle Morton, *The Journey Is Home* (Boston: Beacon Press, 1985), 204-5.

Chapter 11, "In the Middle," Mary E. (Polly) Wheat
1. Henry David Thoreau, *Faith in a Seed: The Dispersion of Seeds and other Late Natural History Writings* (Covelo, CA: Island Press, 1993), epigraph page.
2. Data from *The Woman's Health Data Book: A Profile of Women's Health in the United States* (Washington D.C.: The Jacobs Institute of Women's Health, 1992).

Chapter 13, "Have Some More, Darlings! There's Plenty!,"
Margaret Guenther
1. See chapters 19 and 20.

Chapter 14, "Why Would a Self-Respecting Feminist Be a Christian?,"
Patricia Wilson-Kastner
1. Phyllis Trible, *Texts of Terror* (Philadelphia: Fortress Press, 1984), especially pp. 1-7.

Chapter 15, "From Crisis to Creative Energy," Susan Cole

1. Sophia, or Divine Wisdom, is found in Proverbs 1-9 and Job 26 in the Protestant Old Testament; in Baruch 3-4, Sirach 1, 4, 6, 14-15, 24, and 51, and in Wisdom 6-10 in the Apocrypha; and is even hidden in the New Testament. Her earliest appearance, in Proverbs, shows her claiming divine authority in her power over life and death, her judgment of humanity, her ability to reward and punish, her origin before creation, and her part in it. In Sirach, her divine power, at home in all parts of the cosmos, is celebrated most thoroughly in her rootedness in Israel, where she offers food and drink to those who desire her. In Wisdom, Sophia shines forth as a Spirit who "pervades and permeates all things" (Wisdom 7:24); a "breath of the power of God" (7:25); passing "into holy souls" (7:27). Sophia's divine presence and power informed this later period, closest to the time of Jesus.

Chapter 16, "Spirituality Is About Survival," Marie M. Fortune

1. Bobby McFerrin, "The 23rd Psalm," *Medicine Music* album (Hollywood, CA: Capitol-EMI Music, Inc., 1990).
2. *Ibid.*
3. Maya Angelou, "On the Pulse of Morning" (New York: Random House, 1993).
4. Audre Lorde, "Transformation of Silence," *Sister Outsider: Essays & Speeches* (New York: Crossing Press, 1984), 43; Frances Wood, personal conversation, 1984; Maya Angelou, "On the Pulse of Morning"; Alice Walker, *Revolutionary Petunias & Other Poems* (New York: Harcourt Brace, 1971), 1; Vaclav Havel, "There Is No Godot," *In These Times*, 17, no. 7 (22 Feb. 1993): 24-25; Lee Tai-Young, quoted by Sonia Reid Strawn, *Where There Is No Path: Lee Tai-Young, Her Story* (Seoul, Korea: Korea Legal Aid Center for Family Relations, 1988).
5. Elie Wiesel, *The Oath* (New York: Avon Books, 1974), 44-45.

Chapter 17, "On the Verge of Giving Birth," Carmen Guerrero

1. Matthew Fox, *Original Blessing: A Primer in Creation Spirituality* (Santa Fe, NM: Bear & Co., 1983); *The Coming of the Cosmic Christ* (San Francisco: Harper & Row, 1991); *Creation Spirituality: Liberating Gifts for the People of the Earth* (San Francisco: Harper & Row, 1991).
2. Walter Brueggemann, *Hopeful Imagination: Prophetic Voices in Exile* (Philadelphia: Fortress Press, 1986), 52.

Chapter 18, "Radical Trust," Anne Clarke Brown

1. Elisabeth Schüssler Fiorenza, *But She Said: Feminist Practices of Biblical Interpretation* (Boston: Beacon Press, 1986), 170, 185.

Chapter 19, "Surviving the Second Great Reformation,"
Virginia Ramey Mollenkott

1. Michael Talbot, *The Holographic Universe* (New York: HarperCollins, 1992), 54.
2. *Ibid.*, 17.
3. See Steven Honeygosky, *Milton's House of God* (Columbia, MO: University of Missouri Press, 1993).
4. Alice Walker, *The Color Purple* (New York: Harcourt Brace Jovanovich, 1982).
5. Virginia Ramey Mollenkott, *Sensuous Spirituality: Out from Fundamentalism* (New York: Crossroad, 1992), 41-42.
6. Elisabeth Schüssler Fiorenza, *In Memory of Her* (New York: Crossroad, 1983).

Chapter 20, "Taking the Incarnate God Seriously,"
Elisabeth Moltmann-Wendel

1. Paul Gerhardt (1607-1676), "Ich Steh an deiner Krippenhier." Translated by Elisabeth Moltmann-Wendel.

Chapter 21, "Lead Us Not into Temptation," Mary E. Hunt

1. Nelle Morton, *The Journey Is Home* (Boston: Beacon Press, 1985).

Other LuraMedia Publications

BANKSON, MARJORY ZOET

Braided Streams:
Esther and a Woman's Way of Growing

Seasons of Friendship:
Naomi and Ruth as a Pattern

"This Is My Body. . .":
Creativity, Clay, and Change

BORTON, JOAN

Drawing from the Women's Well: *Reflections on the Life Passage of Menopause*

CARTLEDGE-HAYES, MARY

To Love Delilah:
Claiming the Women of the Bible

DARIAN, SHEA

Seven Times the Sun:
Guiding Your Child through the Rhythms of the Day

DOHERTY, DOROTHY ALBRACHT and McNAMARA, MARY COLGAN

Out of the Skin Into the Soul:
The Art of Aging

DUERK, JUDITH

Circle of Stones:
Woman's Journey to Herself

I Sit Listening to the Wind:
Woman's Encounter within Herself

GOODSON, WILLIAM (with Dale J.)

Re-Souled: *Spiritual Awakenings of a Psychiatrist and his Patient in Alcohol Recovery*

HAGEN, JUNE STEFFENSEN, Editor

Rattling Those Dry Bones:
Women Changing the Church

JEVNE, RONNA FAY

It All Begins With Hope:
Patients, Caretakers, and the Bereaved Speak Out

The Voice of Hope:
Heard Across the Heart of Life

with ALEXANDER LEVITAN
No Time for Nonsense:
Getting Well Against the Odds

KEIFFER, ANN

Gift of the Dark Angel: *A Woman's Journey through Depression toward Wholeness*

LAIR, CYNTHIA

Feeding the Whole Family: *Down-to-Earth Cookbook and Whole Foods Guide*

LODER, TED

Eavesdropping on the Echoes:
Voices from the Old Testament

Guerrillas of Grace:
Prayers for the Battle

Tracks in the Straw:
Tales Spun from the Manger

Wrestling the Light:
Ache and Awe in the Human-Divine Struggle

MEYER, RICHARD C.

One Anothering: *Biblical Building Blocks for Small Groups*

MODJESKA, LEE

Keeper of the Night: *A Portrait of Life in the Shadow of Death*

NELSON, G. LYNN

Writing and Being: *Taking Back Our Lives through the Power of Language*

O'HALLORAN, SUSAN and DELATTRE, SUSAN

The Woman Who Lost Her Heart:
A Tale of Reawakening

PRICE, H.H.

Blackberry Season:
A Time to Mourn, A Time to Heal

RAFFA, JEAN BENEDICT

The Bridge to Wholeness:
A Feminine Alternative to the Hero Myth

Dream Theatres of the Soul:
Empowering the Feminine through Jungian Dreamwork

ROTHLUEBBER, FRANCIS

Nobody Owns Me: *A Celibate Woman Discovers her Sexual Power*

RUPP, JOYCE

The Star in My Heart:
Experiencing Sophia, Inner Wisdom

THOMPSON, G. F.

Slow Miracles: *Urban Women Fighting for Liberation*

WEEMS, RENITA J.

I Asked for Intimacy: *Stories of Blessings, Betrayals, and Birthings*

Just a Sister Away: *A Womanist Vision of Women's Relationships in the Bible*

LuraMedia, Inc.
7060 Miramar Rd., Suite 104
San Diego, CA 92121

LuraMedia™

Books for Healing and Hope,
Balance and Justice
Call 1-800-FOR-LURA for information.